All That Was Ever Ours

Books by Elisabeth Elliot

A Lamp Unto My Feet

All That Was Ever Ours

Be Still My Soul

Discipline

Guided by God's Promises

Journals of Jim Elliot

Joyful Surrender

Keep a Quiet Heart

Love Has a Price Tag

Made for the Journey

The Mark of a Man

Passion and Purity

Quest for Love

Path Through Suffering

On Asking God Why

Secure in the Everlasting Arms

Seeking God's Guidance

Shaping of a Christian Family

A Chance to Die: The Life and Legacy of Amy Carmichael

All That Was Ever Ours

Meditations on Faith and Character

Elisabeth Elliot

Revell
a division of Baker Publishing Group
Grand Rapids, Michigan

Published by Revell Books
a division of Baker Publishing Group
Grand Rapids, Michigan
www.revellbooks.com

Repackaged edition published 2026

ISBN 9780800748807

Printed in the United States of America

Some of the essays in this volume appeared earlier under the title *Twelve Baskets of Crumbs*.

Baker Publishing Group publications use paper produced from sustainable forestry practices and postconsumer waste whenever possible.

26 27 28 29 30 31 32 7 6 5 4 3 2 1

Contents

Foreword

In spite of strong movements in the past few decades, I suspect that what an editor told Dorothy Sayers half a century ago in Britain may apply even now in America: "Our public do not want to be admonished by a woman."

Most of the time I don't want to be admonished by anybody. I'd rather just do what feels good without being told it isn't a good thing to do. When people ask how I *feel* about an issue, it would be easier simply to answer the question instead of getting down to brass tacks and trying to *think* about it. I find that my feelings generally change after I've thought about something, and even if they don't, I'm convinced that thinking rather than feeling should determine my actions.

Here are essays on great themes—Hope, Truth, Freedom, and such. There are essays on lesser themes—nostalgia, boredom, spontaneity. They rise from the everyday life of one individual who tries to *see* things, to *understand* things, to *learn* from them. I try to interpret the meaning of the visible in terms of the Invisible, for it is on that level that all things find their ultimate meaning. As a Christian I believe that all my problems are theological ones—that is, that all have meaning on a level much higher than the level on which I live my life. This idea, of course, is anything but new. It is what Christians have always believed, but many of us do not always live and act as though we believe it. I remember once asking somebody whether he believed a certain thing. "Not specially," was his answer.

I am trying to believe "specially"—in a way, that is, that radically affects everything I do every day of every week. It does make a difference to me that the God who created, names, and numbers the stars in the heavens also numbers the hairs of my head. Such a triviality! I drop quite a few of them in the wastebasket every morning—but God counts them. It makes a difference to me that the God who ordained (which means set in place) the sun, the moon, and all the galaxies, also ordained a worm—to teach a prophet a lesson. He pays attention to very big things and to very small ones. What matters to me matters to Him, and that changes my life.

"You can throw the whole weight of your anxieties upon him, for you are his personal possession," wrote St. Peter, a man who knew quite a bit about anxieties.

The writer to the Hebrew Christians reminded them of Old Testament times when the people of God had a tabernacle in the wilderness, "a holy place in this world for the eternal God" (Hebrews 9:1 Phillips). He mentioned ordinary things—a lamp, a table, loaves of bread, curtains—and extraordinary things: a golden altar and an ark, the cherubim of glory, the mercy seat.

But all were visible and tangible, and all were "full of meaning." My house, my kitchen, my desk, my very body are meant to be holy places in this world for the eternal God. It is from this vantage point that I write.

Because the pieces were written over a period of years, there are occasional irregularities—inevitable repetitions, and the use of tenses which no longer apply, for example when I speak of my mother in the present tense, although she died in 1987. I have made no attempt to expunge or alter these.

—1—

Making Truth Visible

A Talk Given at the Urbana Student Missionary Convention, 1979

More than twenty-three years ago I was living in a small thatch-roofed house in a small jungle clearing on a small river called the Tiwaenu in the small country of Ecuador. An ordinary day would begin anywhere from three o'clock till five or so in the morning. The low crooning of an Auca song would often fit into my dreams for a while before I wakened and then, gradually, I would come to, and hear the Indians, still in their hammocks in the houses around the clearing, singing their strange two- or at most three-note songs:

Waenoni baronki inunae. . . .

I have counted as many as seventy repetitions of verse one, but then, before you lose your mind, they go on to verse two:

MiH baronanai aemumae. . . .

While they were singing I could hear the pat-pat-pat of feather fans as the women fanned the fires, and then the soft cracking sound as they tapped manioc with a stick, peeled and split it in preparation for cooking. They would push the glowing log-tips together, set their clay pots on top, and I would hear the pfff-pfff as they blew on the fire. Roosters would crow, the fanning and the songs would go on, and as dawn broke behind the tall trees I would give up pretending to be asleep. I would open my eyes and the two teen-aged boys who slept in the house next door (our houses had no walls) would belt out the first announcement of the day: "Baru! Nani omaemunamba!" which means, "She's awake!"

I was a freak to these people. They were the Auca Indians of the Ecuadorian rain forest, a people so isolated that most of them had never laid eyes on anybody they didn't know, so primitive they still made fire with two sticks. They wore no clothes at all, only a piece of cotton string around the hips. When I asked what the string was for they looked at me horrified. "Well, you certainly wouldn't expect us to go around naked, would you?" They had a notion from way back—nobody could tell me where they got it—that everybody in the world who wasn't an Auca was a cannibal, so when they met up with strangers they usually dispatched them as quickly as possible with eight-foot wooden spears to avoid ending up in the strangers' cooking pot.

One day, two years before I lived there, the Aucas had found five white men on a little strip of sand on the Curaray River, men who had been dropping gifts to them from a yellow airplane. The Indians called the plane *ibu*, meaning bumblebee, because the sound it made was almost identical. They had argued among themselves for a long time about whether these men might be as friendly as they appeared to be, shouting and gesticulating from the plane, or whether they were just masters of treachery and deception. They couldn't possibly know that they were missionaries, bent only on giving them some very good news. When they finally found themselves face to face on the sandstrip, the Indians hesitated, uncertain as to what to do. At last, the oldest of the six men, a man whom I later got to know as Gikita, said, "Well, I brought my spear—butu Wati! taenumu waeninani yaeae—I'm going to kill them," and with that he lunged across the river that separated them and sank his weapon into the back of one of the missionaries. A long fight ensued but ended with all five of the Americans dead.

That happened more than twenty-five years ago. Maybe it seems unusual in the twentieth century, maybe it seems strange that the God whom the five served should allow them to be defeated by a handful of utterly misled, totally ignorant Indians to whom spearing was all in a day's work. But in Christian history the story is neither unusual nor strange. In fact, it seems legitimate to me to add the names of those men—Ed, Roj, Nate, Pete, and Jim—to a long list given to us in the Book of Hebrews. You remember many of those who qualified for the great gallery of chapter 11: Noah, Abraham, Moses, David, Samuel, and the prophets—even a harlot named Rahab.

There were those not named who conquered kingdoms, shut the mouths of lions, quenched the furious blaze of fire, and escaped from death. They were the successful ones—the winners, you'd say. But do you remember the list at the end of the chapter? You never saw any pictures of them in your Sunday-school papers. They were the ones who were tortured, mocked, flogged, chained, or stoned to death. There were some, the story says, who were sawn in two. They're in the same list, remember, right in there with the winners.

We'd call them martyrs. You know what the Bible calls them? Witnesses. Greek students know it's the same word. The word for witness is *marturia*. So in God's categories it really doesn't matter whether, humanly speaking, you win or lose, whether you're a victim or a victor. You're a witness.

I started by telling you about my experience of living with people who regarded me as a freak. I was some kind of nut to them. I had hair like palm fiber, they said. Eyes like a jaguar's—blue ones, altogether the wrong color for a *person* to have. To a people whose skin was the beautiful shade of strong tea, mine was pathetically washed-out. I was a head taller than anybody. Before they saw me they had heard that a very tall foreigner was coming so they built me a house about twenty feet tall. It was an awful letdown for them when I showed up, only five foot nine. But everything about me was weird. Everything I did was bizarre. I didn't know how to do anything useful like planting manioc or making clay pots or weaving hammocks or catching fish with my hands, and when I tried, my daughter Valerie, who was three and had learned their language almost overnight, would yell, "Kyae akam!" which means, "Everybody get a load of this!"

Day after day the women and most of the children would go off to the plantations to work and the men would go hunting. There I would be, sitting in a hammock with my notebooks and file box, scratching the gnat bites, blinking the smoke out of my eyes, trying to figure out a language nobody had even written down. Phrases like *Wuru naimae nano kaewuti ani*. Or *MMm wa*—which means, "It stinks."

In the evenings everybody came home, the women from the planting, the men from hunting. They cooked and ate whatever they had brought—manioc, plantains, birds, monkeys, tapirs, whatever. They went to sleep very early and there I'd still be, sitting in the hammock, Valerie asleep in a blanket on a slab of split bamboo beside me. I'd fan my fire, scratch bug bites, study a little bit sometimes, but candles were hard to come by down there, so I would think and pray.

One of the things I thought most about was witnessing. That's why I was there—to witness. It had to mean something besides giving out tracts, speaking to people in gas stations, going from door to door. Those were perfectly valid activities, but the application seemed too limited. One day I found a verse which altered my understanding: "'My witnesses,' says the Lord, 'are you, my servants, you whom I have chosen to know me and put your faith in me and understand that I am he.'"

I realized I had been chosen to know him. A witness must first of all know something. God's witnesses know him, put faith in him, understand who he is. In the first letter of John he says, "We are writing to you about something which has always existed, yet which we ourselves actually saw and heard, something which we had opportunity to observe closely and even to hold in our hands, and yet, as we know now, was something of the very Word of Life Himself." John knew what he was talking about.

What are we talking about? Whom are we talking about? We have got to know him. Jesus made it very clear that there is only one route to that knowledge: obedience. "If a man loves me he obeys me and I will make myself known to him."

You must *know* him. You must *see* him. You must *hear* his words. That makes you a witness, just as seeing an accident at a street corner makes you a witness. Then what does a witness do? You might be called into court to testify. Leviticus 5 says, "If a person hears a solemn adjuration to give evidence as a witness to something he has seen or heard and does not declare what he knows, he commits a sin and must accept responsibility." The Apostle John came, the Gospel tells us, to witness to the Light. He was not the Light. He came to give evidence. Another faithful witness was Christ himself. By everything he said or did he gave evidence—he was evidence of what the Father was like. He spoke only what he heard the Father say.

A witness speaks. His witness is his word. But it is also his life. Witness is action. It makes truth visible. God instructed Moses to make a special kind of tent in the wilderness, gave him specific details about dimensions, materials, and furnishings, even down to the silver hooks and bronze pegs, the colors of the embroidery on the waistband of the priests' vestments. God did this to make truth visible. It was to give the people tangible evidence of intangible verities.

The disciples observed Jesus' actions and saw the manifestation of Truth, the Word made flesh, visible and comprehensible. Then, when it was time for the disciples to take over where he left off, he promised that they would receive power and become witnesses. The process has been the same ever since: we see him, we are given power, we become witnesses. Some of those mentioned in Hebrews did just that. There was Noah. What an assignment he had—to build that huge boat, of an unheard of size and shape, on dry land where there wasn't the smallest chance of ever hauling it to any place where it could float. Imagine what the neighbors thought! Poor old Noah, he's gone bananas. But he kept his cool. The account says he built it reverently. It also says his action "condemned the unbelief of the rest of the world." That's one of the things a faithful witness does.

What about Abraham? His name is on the list for several reasons, one of them being his willingness to make a human sacrifice. It was the very son through whom God was to fulfill his tremendous promise that God was now asking him to offer up. Imagine the silent journey up the mountain, the old man who had gotten up early in the morning to obey God, the donkey carrying the load of wood, the boy, perhaps ten or twelve years old, and the two servants. When the father and son had left the servants behind, the boy spoke at last. "Father."

"What is it, my son?"

"Here are the fire and the wood, but where is the animal for sacrifice?"

"God will provide it."

And they went on in silence. In silence too, I imagine, they set about building an altar and arranging the wood. I wonder what happened next. I wonder if either of them said anything. I try and try to visualize that scene in the lonely spot on the mountain in the wilderness, the father who had known God's leading through so many vicissitudes, in a desperate conflict of desire to be a faithful son to his Heavenly Father and a faithful father to his earthly son.

I picture not only the life-and-death struggle on the mountaintop but also the throngs of angelic beings, poised, attentive, leaning, as it were, in breathless stillness over the scene. Isaac, helpless and incredulous, looks at his father. The angels wait for the old patriarch's decision. Is his trust in God strong enough to enable him actually to slit the boy's throat? Will he by his obedience witness to belief, or by disobedience to unbelief? The decision matters infinitely—not only to the old man and the boy, not only to God who gave the command, not only to the cloud of witnesses who watch, but to all the world for all time. It matters to you and me.

They wait. Abraham stretches out his hand. His fingers close around the hilt of the knife. Suddenly the voice of the angel of the Lord: "Abraham!"

"Here I am."

"Don't touch him. Now I know that you are a God-fearing man. You have not withheld from me your son. All nations on earth shall pray to be blessed as your descendants are blessed, and this because you have obeyed me."

Witnessing means obedience. Every time you do what God says to do or refuse to do what he says not to do you witness to the truth. And witnessing to the truth is a very risky business—risky in the world's terms. You're likely to be arrested, Jesus predicted, handed over to prison, brought before governors and kings "for my name's sake. This will be your chance to witness for me. You will be betrayed . . . some of you will be killed." Solzhenitsyn, Dietrich Bonhoeffer, Corrie ten Boom, and thousands of others know what he meant. They also understand what he said next: "Hold on, and you will win your souls. In the world you'll have tribulation, but cheer up, I have overcome the world."

Witnessing conquers the world. But it doesn't exempt you from suffering.

Daniel was a man who was willing to stand up and be counted. His witness was so pure that jealous ministers and satraps knew they would never find any charge against him unless they could find one in his religion. They found it. He was a praying man, and when he heard the decree that he was to quit praying he decided to be judicious and say his prayers on the golf course with his eyes open. Is that what it says? No. Daniel knelt by his window facing Jerusalem three times a day, exactly as he had always done, and of course they got him. The king gave the order and Daniel was hurled into a pit of hungry lions. The king had a very bad night—couldn't eat, couldn't sleep, couldn't even enjoy his harem. But Daniel had a wonderful night. The lions were there, but so was the angel of God. "No trace of injury was found on him," the story says, "because he had put his faith in his God." God didn't keep him out of the pit. He went into it with him. The world says, "What is faith? Show us." Daniel showed us.

Witness enables others to see what they could not otherwise have seen. It changes the picture. Think of Stephen. He never minced any words. Standing before the highest civil and religious court of the Jewish nation, called the Sanhedrin, he witnessed. He spoke the plain truth about Israel's history: "You obstinate people, heathen in your thinking, heathen in the way you are listening to me now, it's always the same. You never fail to resist the Holy Spirit. You who have received the law of God miraculously by the hand of angels, you are the men who have disobeyed it!"

If miracles didn't persuade them, what would Stephen's defiance do? They ground their teeth at him in a rage and stoned him to death. But while the rocks were flying, Stephen saw something. He saw heaven opened, he saw the glory of God, and Jesus himself standing at his right hand. That's witness. It conquers the world. It makes truth visible. It changes the picture.

When we see Stephen we see not the fury of the religious Jews, not the rain of stones falling on his head, but a man beholding the Lord. Faith stands in the midst of suffering and sees glory. The Church is here not to deliver us from suffering—and I believe you young men and women will be called to suffer—the Church will not deliver you from it, but will make witnesses, those who see beyond things like an ark, a sacrifice, a lion's den, a furnace—those who see the promises of God, the angel in the lion's den, the Son of Man in the flames, Jesus standing up to welcome his beloved Stephen.

A witness clarifies alternatives. Pope John Paul, pressed to slacken the rule against the ordination of women, beleaguered by women who preach a spurious doctrine of freedom, has clarified the alternatives. Faithful to the Gospel, he replied simply that the issue was not one of human rights but of the will of God.

In a suburb of Moscow a priest named Dmitri Dudko held dialogues every Sunday in his church. It is a very dangerous thing to speak out for Christ in Russia today and people came and put to him all kinds of hard questions—is it all right, for example, to emigrate to the West? "When you run away from difficulties," Father Dudko replied, "you run away from Christ's cross." Somebody asked why God had to be crucified, when God should be all-powerful. "You have a modern understanding of power, force, the thunder of artillery. But our God is a God of love, and he chose the Cross as the weapon of our salvation," the priest said. "One must choose either the kingdom of God or absurdity." Hear his witness.

There's an amazing word at the end of the chapter in Hebrews. "It was not God's plan that they should reach perfection without us." Noah, Abraham, Daniel and his friends, Stephen, the five missionaries in Ecuador—they won't reach perfection—*without us*? That's what it says. So what are we supposed to do? The Book tells us.

"Surrounded then as we are by these serried ranks of witnesses, let us strip off everything that hinders us as well as the sin that dogs our feet and let us run the race that we have to run with patience, our eyes fixed on Jesus the Source and the Goal of our faith."

The race *we* have to run. Not Noah's or Abraham's. God chooses different tests—he writes different exams for each of us, exactly suited to prove the quality of our faith. If to be his witness means for you flunking a course because you refuse to cheat the way everybody else is doing, if it means losing money because you're conscientious about paying your income tax when you know you could fudge a little bit, if it means looking like a freak or a square or a Victorian or a nerd—will you stand up and be counted? Strip off what hinders you, the verse says. You know what it is. Fear, perhaps. Of what? Suffering? Embarrassment? Maybe your hindrance is love of comfort—America's idea of suffering is having to put the thermostat down a few degrees. What is the "sin that dogs our feet"? Gluttony? Irresponsibility? Procrastination? Old-fashioned selfishness? What's your list? Strip it off. Get rid of it. Run your race, eyes fixed on the Source and Goal—Jesus, who endured a cross.

Remember these serried ranks of witnesses that surround us. Remember that they're cheering for you. Remember the word that was made so powerful to me back there in that thatched house: "My witnesses," says the Lord, "are you, my servants, you whom I have chosen to know Me and put your faith in Me and understand that I am He."

2

Hope Is a Fixed Anchor

My friend Miriam is herself a walking miracle, having recovered more than twenty years ago from cancer. Her case was so serious that the doctors told her husband not to expect her home from the hospital. The cure was so miraculous that one doctor described it this way: "If you parked your car on a hill and the brakes let go, would you expect it to roll to the top of the hill? That's how incredible this is. This cancer was supposed to travel in one direction and kill her. It went the opposite way and quit."

Miriam was the only one who could talk like a Dutch uncle to my husband when he had cancer. He would listen to her when he did not want to hear a word out of the rest of us. His hope, of course, was that he would be cured as she had been.

The more hopeless my husband's case appeared to be, the more faithfully Miriam called to remind me, "Our hope, Elisabeth, is not in radiation or surgery or chemotherapy. Our hope is not in the doctors. Our hope is in *God*."

One night when I went to bed I found a card on my pillow. My daughter Valerie, still a teenager, had made it, intertwining the letters with tiny colored flowers. It said HOPE IN THE LORD. With all my heart I did that. With all my heart I prayed. It has been eight years now since Add died, and the card is before me tonight as I write. I am still hoping—but for what?

Christian hope is a different sort of thing from other kinds. The Greek word used in the New Testament for hope was one which in classical literature could mean expectation of good or bad, but was used by Christians to mean that in which one confides, or to which one flees for refuge. The real essence of the word is *trust*.

When Lazarus died, the hopes of his two loving sisters, Mary and Martha, were dashed. Jesus, hearing the news, did not hurry to the house but stayed where he was for two more days. When he finally got to Bethany both sisters greeted him with the same words: "If only you had been here, Lord!" Martha remembered the fact of the resurrection. She knew Lazarus would rise again on the last day, but that wasn't really good enough. She wanted her brother *now*, and her brother was dead. The terrible thing was that he might have been alive if only Jesus had been there. Jesus said to her, "I myself am the resurrection."

This is our hope. It is a living thing. It is, in fact, Christ himself. It is also something to live by. When our hopes for healing or success or the solution to a problem or freedom from financial distress seem to come to nothing, we feel just as Mary and Martha did. Jesus might have done something about it but he didn't. We lie awake thinking about all the "if onlys." We wonder if it is somehow our fault that the thing didn't work. We doubt whether prayer is of any use after all. Is God up there? Is he listening? Does he care?

The Lord might very well have healed my husband's disease as wonderfully as he healed Miriam's. The simple fact is that he didn't.

HOPE IN THE LORD, says the little card. How am I to do that now? By placing my confidence in the God who promises faithfulness. He has far better things up his sleeve than we imagine. Mary and Martha had envisioned his coming and raising a sick man from his bed. He came too late. Unfortunately Lazarus was dead—so dead, Martha pointed out, that decomposition would have set in. It had not crossed their minds that they were about to see an even more astonishing thing than the one they had hoped for—a swaddled corpse answering the Master's call and walking, bound and muffled, out of the tomb.

The only difference I see in the Lazarus story and our twentieth-century stories of disappointed hopes is the matter of time. Jesus did arrive at Mary and Martha's in a matter of a couple of days, and in perhaps an hour or so after his arrival he raised Lazarus. It looks very quick and easy as we read the story, but of course the two sisters experienced all that those who love a sick person experience, and all the agony of bereavement. Sorrow ran its course. They suffered what humans always suffer, albeit for a very short time.

The truth of the story is that God knew what was happening. Nothing was separating the grieving women from his love. He heard their prayers, counted their tears, held his peace. *But he was faithful, and he was at work.* He had a grand miracle in mind. The Jews who saw Jesus weep were baffled, and said just what we would have said: "Could he not have kept this man from dying if he could open that blind man's eyes?"

God's timing of the events of our world is engineered from the eternal silence. One time he heals a sick man, such as the paralytic who was lowered through a roof. Another time he lets a sick man die. Miriam's cancer receded. Add's cancer grew. Was God paying attention in the one case but not in the other? So it seemed to Mary and Martha at first. Their prayers for healing were not answered. Jesus did not come. Lazarus died. But what a glorious ending to their story! And ours? What about ours?

"Did I not tell you," Jesus asked, "that if you believed, you would see the wonder of what God can do?" Here is the clue to the lesson: It is faith he is looking for, a quiet confidence that whatever it is he is up to, it will be a wonderful thing, never mind the timing, never mind whether it is what we have been asking for.

The usual notion of hope is a particular outcome: physical healing, for example. The Christian notion, on the other hand, is a manner of life. I rest the full weight of my hopes on Christ himself, who not only raised the dead but was himself raised, and says to me in the face of all deaths, "I myself am the resurrection." The duration of my suffering may be longer than that of Lazarus's sisters, but if I believe, trust, flee to God for refuge, I am safe even in my sorrow, I am held by the confidence of God's utter trustworthiness. He is at work, producing miracles I haven't imagined. I must wait for them. The Book of the Revelation describes some of them. The intricacies of his sovereign will and the pace at which he effects it ("deliberate speed, majestic instancy") are beyond me now, but I am sure his plan is in operation.

HOPE IN THE LORD. Doctors, chemotherapy, surgery, radiation might very well have been a part of God's plan, methods he might have used to answer our prayers for a complete cure for my husband. They evidently were not. But that was not where our hopes really lay. They lay then, as they lie now, on the faithfulness of the One who died for us and rose again.

What God promised to Abraham ("Surely blessing I will bless thee") he promises to us. We have two "utterly immutable things, the word of God and the oath of God, who cannot lie," according to the Book of Hebrews. Therefore we who are refugees from this dying world have a source of strength. We can grasp "the hope he holds out to us. This hope we hold as the utterly reliable anchor for our souls, fixed in the innermost shrine of Heaven, where Jesus has already entered on our behalf" (6:19, 20 Phillips).

I don't know, when I'm asking for something here on earth, what is going on in the innermost shrine of Heaven (I like to think about it, though). I am sure of one thing: it is good. Because Jesus is there. Jesus loves me. Jesus has gone into that shrine on my behalf. The hope we have is a living hope, an unassailable one. We wait for it, in faith and patience. Christ is the resurrection and the life. No wonder Easter is the greatest of Christian feast days! No wonder Christians sing!

> The powers of death have done
> their worst,
> But Christ their legions hath
> dispersed:
> Let shout of holy joy outburst.
> Alleluia!
> The three sad days are quickly
> sped,
> He rises glorious from the dead:
> All glory to our risen Head!
> Alleluia!
> Lord! By the stripes which
> wounded thee,
> From death's dread sting thy
> servants free,
> That we may live and sing to thee.
> Alleluia!
> Latin 1695—Episcopal Hymnal

—3—

But I Don't *Feel* Called

A seminary student stopped me a few days ago to ask the question that troubles many young people today. It is not new. I struggled with it when I was a student, as I suppose people have for many centuries. "How can I tell if God is calling me? I don't really *feel* called."

Usually the question refers to a life's work. Nobody seems to stew very much about whether God is calling them to run down to the grocery store or take in a movie. We need groceries. We like movies. If the refrigerator is empty or there's a good movie in town, we jump into the car and go. Even Christians do this. Spiritual "giants" do it, I guess. They don't even pray about it. But this matter of the *mission field*. Oh, God, do you want me *there*? Shall I risk everything and launch out to some third world backwater, some waterless desert, some dreadful place where there are starving children, refugees, Marxists, dictators? Are you asking me to drag my wife, my children, to a place like that?

The call of God to Saul of Tarsus was dramatic—he was blinded, knocked flat, and clearly spoken to. God got his attention. But later in Antioch the Holy Spirit spoke to certain prophets and teachers. "Set apart Barnabas and Saul for me, to do the work to which I have called them." That was good enough. Barnabas and Saul obeyed the divine call, even though it came through other men.

It was during the Mass of the Feast of St. Matthias, in a chapel in the midst of a great, silent forest, that Francis of Assisi heard the call of God. It was not through an angel or a disembodied voice from beyond, but through the reading of the Gospel for that day: "Go and preach the message, 'The Kingdom of Heaven is at hand!' . . . Freely you have received, freely give." When the young man heard the words read by the priest, he felt that God had finally illumined his path. He did not, however, trust his feelings. He asked the priest to explain the passage. The priest said that Christ's disciples were to preach repentance everywhere, to take nothing with them, and to trust God alone to supply their needs.

> Francis thrilled with happiness at this revelation and exclaimed enthusiastically: "That is what I want! That is what I seek! That is what I long to do with all my heart!" On the instant, he threw away his staff, took off his shoes, and laid aside his cloak, keeping only a tunic; replaced his leather belt with a cord, and made himself a rough garment, so poor and so badly cut that it could inspire envy in no man.
>
> Omer Englebert
> *St. Francis of Assisi*

There are at least six lessons in this short story:

1. The man wanted God's direction.
2. He went to church, where he could hear godly preaching.
3. He listened to the Word of God.

4. He asked for help from one who was his spiritual superior.
5. He accepted the help.
6. He acted at once.

It is significant that he found in the words of the Lord the answer to a deep longing in his heart.

In C. S. Lewis's *Preface to Paradise Lost*, he describes Aeneas' unfaltering search for the "abiding city," his willingness to pay the terrible price to reach it at last, even though he casts a wistful side-glance at those not called as he is. "This is the very portrait of a vocation: a thing that calls or beckons, that calls inexorably, yet you must strain your ears to catch the voice, that insists on being sought, yet refuses to be found." Then there were the Trojan women who had heard the call, yet refused to follow all the way, and wept on the Sicilian shore. "To follow the vocation does not mean happiness," Lewis writes, "but once it has been heard, there is no happiness for those who do not follow."

Yes. My heart says yes to that. What agonies I suffered as a young woman, straining my ears to catch the voice, full of fear that I would miss it, yet longing to hear it, longing to be told what to do, in order that I might do it. That desire is a pure one. Most of our desires are tainted at least a little, but the desire to do the will of God surely is our highest. Is it reasonable to think that God would not finally reveal his will to us? Is it (we must also ask) reasonable *not* to use our powers of reason, given to us by him? Does it make more sense to go to the grocery store because groceries are needed than to go to foreign lands because workers are needed? If we deny the simple logic of going where the need is most desperate, we may, like the Trojan women, spend the rest of our lives suspended

Twixt miserable longing for the
present land
And the far realms that call them
by the fates' command.
Aeneid, V, 656

While Virgil wrote of mythical heroes, his lines echo the more ancient lines of the Psalms which are rich with assurances of God's faithful guidance of those who honestly desire it, and of the lasting rewards of obedience.

Happy the men whose refuge is in thee,
whose hearts are set on the pilgrim ways!
The Lord will hold back no good thing
from those whose life is blameless.
84:5, 11 NEB

Very near is the Lord to those
who call to him, in singleness of heart.
He fulfills their desire if only they fear him.
145:18, 19 NEB

It is the sixth lesson from the St. Francis story that is most often overlooked. Obedience is action. Often we do not have any instant light on the particular question we've been asking God, but he has shown us *something* we ought to do. Whatever it is, however unrelated it may seem to the "big" decision, do it. Do it at once. We thus put ourselves in the path of God's will. A single step taken, if we have his Word as a lamp for our feet, throws sufficient light for the next step. Following the Shepherd we learn, like sheep, to know his voice. We will become acquainted with his call and will not follow a stranger's.

—4—

The Comfort of Discipline

Hate is a strong word, but in the context of biblical discipline, could it be that too many parents today hate their children? We saw it a couple of weeks ago, and in church at that. Lars and I attended a very small church where there was a very large number of small children. The creaking of pews, rustling of books and papers, dropping of crayons and toys and offering-plate nickels, talking, crying, and traipsing up and down the aisles for trips to the rest room all made it quite impossible to listen to the sermon. One child who was sitting with his father in front of us was passed forward over the back of the pew to his mother. Immediately he wanted daddy. Back over the pew again, headfirst into his father's lap. In a few minutes, up to mommy. So it went.

A week later we went to a much larger church with over a hundred children present. They were quiet. We were amazed and later questioned a couple who were members there. "We believe Christian parents should control their children," they said simply. Where did they get that idea, we wanted to know. Well, from the Bible. The Book of Proverbs speaks repeatedly of the use of the rod. One reference is in chapter 13: "A father who spares the rod hates his son, but one who loves him keeps him in order." The implication is clear: The keeping of order, where children are concerned, sometimes requires the use of the rod.

In the small church, it seemed, they hated their children. In the big one they loved them. They were taught (from the pulpit, the couple told us) to love them according to the Bible's definition of love: Keep them in order.

My dear friend Mari, the wife of a Welsh shepherd, writes often about lessons she learns from watching sheep. In a letter to me she described a very hard winter:

> All the sheep were brought down from the mountain early, about one thousand breeding ewes. Two hundred are wintering in a lowland farm while the others are hand-fed here with hay and maize. The grass is covered with snow. . . . When John wants to move sheep or cows from one pasture to another it is a hopeless job when the lambs or calves take to running their own way. They will be followed invariably by their mothers, who will go headlong after their offspring, blindly, in their care for them. What chaos! If only the parents would stay where they were, holding their ground, defending their standpoint, the little ones would eventually return to them and would willingly be led together to the right place.
>
> Although our men are fighting hard against nature's elements these days, even that's easier than fighting unchanged, selfish human nature. I wonder: are the sheep and cows a true picture of what's happening in the world? Road men refuse to grit and salt the snow-covered roads; dustmen, gravediggers, and others are pressing for more money. It is so true that money is the source of all evils. If it isn't the capitalists, it's the workers. This has been true in every generation. But now parents are leaning over backwards to please their children, afraid of displeasing them. Teachers live in fear of their pupils at school, bosses are afraid of the workers, the government of trade unions. It's anarchy.

Anarchy is the complete absence of order and authority. It's what lambs and calves like. It's what people like too—for themselves. (It's another matter when the neighbors scorn order and authority.) A Houston high school principal described the new educational system as a "cross-graded, multi-ethnic, individualized, open-ended learning program with the main objective being to learn respect for the uniqueness of a person." Maybe that's what the parents in the little church were aiming for. It was open-ended, all right, and each unique little individual was doing his or her not particularly unique thing. The result was chaos, if not downright anarchy. A short lesson, emphasized in the vestibule with a narrow "board of education," i.e., a rod, might have done wonders to teach small individuals respect for the persons around them, who were there not to provide an audience for their antics but to worship.

The trouble starts, of course, not when the kids tumble out of the station wagon and charge into church. It starts at home, before they can walk, with parents who believe that love means giving them what they want and letting them do what they choose. They don't like ordinary food. They blow it out when they're babies and throw it on the floor or down the garbage grinder later on. They scream for other foods, and their screams are rewarded. If screams don't do the trick, tantrums will, especially in public. (Watch them around the gumball machine in any supermarket. The initial "No" is quickly reversed.) A child who doesn't throw tantrums can use another weapon—he can go into a sulk. His parents pity him and this teaches him to pity himself. When things don't go his way he knows that he has a right to resentment. The spiritual implications in later life of this kind of early training are disastrous: "If God loves me he will give me what I want. If he does not give me what I want he does not love me." That isn't what the Bible teaches, of course, but it's what a child may conclude if his parents operate this way.

Training children, like corralling calves and lambs, is a great deal of trouble. It takes sacrifice. It's much easier to let them go. But you can't do that if you care about them. Only the one who cares about them will go to the trouble of bringing them under control. "The good shepherd gives his life for the sheep." The sheep don't take kindly to the crook he uses, to the dogs who herd them where they don't want to go, or to the disinfectant baths they are plunged into. It is the shepherd's sole purpose to take care of them, to see to their well-being according to *his* wisdom, not according to *their* whims.

My parents loved us enough to make us wear galoshes (those awful things with black metal clasps) when "nobody else had to wear them"; to see to it that we got five meals a day (three for the body and two for the soul, the latter including hymns, Bible reading, and prayer); to say no to things like candy or coming in when we felt like it, or skipping piano lessons and church; to give us chores to do around the house and to make it clear that if we didn't do them they wouldn't get done; to give us an allowance even during the Depression and teach us that some of it belonged to God; to stick by what they had said—line upon line, precept upon precept, here a little and there a little. They drew lines. We knew where they were drawn. They didn't move them. They knew more about life than we did and had a fairly clear picture of what was good for us. Like other kids we complained that they didn't love us or they would do so-and-so. "When you have children of your own," Mother would often say, "you can let them do that if you want to." She knew we wouldn't want to—if we loved them.

We've got it backwards—love says don't restrain, hate says restrain. God puts it the other way: "The Lord disciplines him *whom he loves*, and chastises every son whom he receives . . . If you are left without discipline . . . then you are illegitimate children and not sons" (Hebrews 12:6, 8 RSV). "When we fall under the Lord's judgment, he is disciplining us, *to save us* from being condemned with the rest of the world" (1 Cor. 11:32 NEB).

It is not difficult for adults to see what's wrong with other parents and other people's children. But how blind we are in our childish reactions to the dealings of a kind Heavenly Father! The motive for discipline is love. Its purpose is salvation. The people of Israel muttered treason against him and said, "It was because the Lord hated us that he brought us out of Egypt" (Deuteronomy 1:27 NEB). Freed from slavery, they missed onions. Led by the Lord of Hosts himself with his angels and a pillar of cloud and fire, they were terrified of the Amorites. "You saw how the Lord your God carried you all the way to this place as a father carries his son. In spite of this you did not trust the Lord your God" (verse 32).

Discipline or "chastening" can be a painful thing for us poor mortals. We think only of the "rod" itself—the hard experience, the prayer that was answered with a No, the shattered hope, the misunderstanding, the blow to pride—forgetting the loving Hand that administers the lesson and the Savior who like a shepherd leads us. We forget how much we need his tender care.

As parents, let us faithfully remember that the keeping of order sometimes requires the use of the rod. As children of the Father and sheep of his pasture, let us remember humbly to accept his discipline, praying:

We are Thine, do Thou befriend
us, be the Guardian of our way;
Keep Thy flock, from sin defend us,
seek us when we go astray.

— 5 —

On Asking God Why

One of the things I am no longer as good at as I used to be is sleeping through the night. I'm rather glad about that, for there is something pleasant about waking in the small hours and realizing that one is, in fact, in bed and need not get up. One can luxuriate. Between two and three o'clock yesterday morning I luxuriated.

I lay listening to the night sounds in a small house on the "stem and rockbound" coast of Massachusetts. The wind whistled and roared, wrapping itself around the house and shaking it. On the quarter hours the clock in the living room softly gave out Whittington's chime. I could hear the tiny click as the electric blanket cut off and on, the cracking of the cold in the walls, the expensive rumble of the oil burner beneath me, and the reassuring rumble of a snoring husband beside me. Underneath it all was the deep, drumming rhythm of the surf, synchronized with the distant bellow of "Mother Ann's Cow," the name given the sounding buoy that guards the entrance to Gloucester Harbor.

I was thinking, as I suppose I am always thinking, in one way or another, about mystery. An English magazine which contained an interview with me had just come in the mail, and of course I read it, not to find out what I'd said to the man last spring in Swanwick, but to find out what he said I'd said. He had asked me about some of the events in my life, and I had told him that because of them I had had to "come to terms with mystery." That was an accurate quotation, I'm sure, but as I lay in bed I knew that one never comes to any final terms with mystery—not in this life, anyway. We keep asking the same unanswerable questions and wondering why the explanations are not forthcoming. We doubt God. We are anxious about everything when we have been told quite clearly to be anxious about nothing. Instead of stewing we are supposed to pray and give thanks.

Well, I thought, *I'll have a go at it*. I prayed about several things for which I could not give thanks. But I gave thanks in the middle of each of those prayers because I was still sure (the noise of wind and ocean were reminding me) that underneath are the everlasting arms.

My prayers embraced four things:

1. Somebody I love is gravely ill.
2. Something I wanted has been denied.
3. Something I worked very hard for failed.
4. Something I prized is lost.

I can be specific about three of the things. A letter from a friend of many years describes her cancer surgery and its aftermath—an incision that had to be scraped and cleaned daily for weeks.

> It was so painful that Diana, Jim, Monica, and I prayed while she cleaned it, three times and some days four times. Monica would wipe my tears. Yes, Jesus stands right there as the pain takes my breath away and my toes curl to keep from crying out

loud. But I haven't asked, Why me, Lord? It is only now that I can pray for cancer patients and know how the flesh hurts and how relief, even for a moment, is blessed.

The second thing is a manuscript on which I have spent years. It is not, I believe, publishable now, and I can see no way to redeem it. It feels as though those years of work have gone down the drain. Have they? What ought I to do about this failure?

The other thing is my J. B. Phillips translation of the New Testament, given to me when I lived in the jungle in 1960 and containing nineteen years' worth of notes. I left this book on an airplane between Dallas and Atlanta several weeks ago. The stewardess brought my breakfast as I was reading it, so I laid it in my lap and spread my napkin on top of it. I suppose it slipped down beside the seat. (Stupid of me, of course, but on the same trip my husband did just as stupid a thing. He left his briefcase on the sidewalk outside the terminal. We prayed, and the prayers were almost instantly answered. Someone had picked the briefcase up and turned it in to the airline, and we had it back in a couple of hours.) I am lost without my Phillips. I feel crippled. It is as though a large segment of the history of my spiritual pilgrimage has been obliterated. It was the one New Testament in which I knew my way around. I knew where things were on the page and used it constantly in public speaking because I could refer quickly to passages I needed. What shall I do?

I have done the obvious things. Prayer is the first thing—asking God to do what I *can't* do. The second thing is to get busy and do what I *can* do. I prayed for my friend, of course, and then I sat down and wrote her a letter. I don't know what else to do for her now. My husband and I prayed together about the lost New Testament (and many of my friends prayed too). We went to the proper authorities at the airline and have been assured that everything will be done to recover it, but it has not turned up. We prayed about the bad manuscript and asked for editorial advice. It looks quite irremediable. I continue to pray repeatedly, extensively, and earnestly about all of the above. And one more thing: I seek the lessons God wants to teach me, and that means that I ask why.

There are those who insist that it is a very bad thing to question God. To them, "why?" is a rude question. That depends, I believe, on whether it is an honest search, in faith, for his meaning, or whether it is the challenge of unbelief and rebellion. The psalmist often questioned God and so did Job. God did not answer the questions, but he answered the man—with the mystery of himself.

He has not left us entirely in the dark. We know a great deal more about his purposes than poor old Job did, yet Job trusted him. He is not only the Almighty—Job's favorite name for him. He is also our Father, and what a father does is not by any means always understood by the child. If he loves the child, however, the child trusts him. It is the child's ultimate good that the father has in mind. Terribly elementary. Yet I have to be reminded of this when, for example, my friend suffers, when a book I think I can't possibly do without is lost, when a manuscript is worthless.

The three things are not all in the same category. The second and third things have to do with my own carelessness and failure. Yet in all three I am reminded that God is my Father still, that he does have a purpose for me, and that nothing, absolutely nothing, is useless in the fulfillment of that purpose if I'll trust him for it and submit to the lessons.

"God disciplines us for our good *that we may share his holiness*." That is a strong clue to the explanation we are always seeking. God's purpose for us is holiness—his own holiness which we are to share—and the sole route to that end is discipline.

Discipline very often involves loss, diminishment, "failings from us, vanishings." Why? Because God wills our perfection in holiness, that is, our *joy*. But, we argue, why should diminishments be the prerequisite for joy? The answer to that lies within the great mystery that underlies creation: the principle of life out of death, exemplified for all time in the Incarnation ("that a vile Manger his low Bed should prove, who in a Throne of stars Thunders above," as Crashaw expressed it) and in the cross and resurrection ("who, for the joy that was set before him, endured a cross"). Christ's radical diminishments—his birth as a helpless baby and his death as a common criminal—accomplished our salvation.

It follows that if we are to share in his destiny we must share in his death, which means, for us sinners, the willingness to offer up to him not only ourselves but all that goes with that gift, including the simplest, down-to-earth things. These things may be aggravating and irritating and humiliating as well as mysterious. But it is the very aggravation and irritation and humiliation that we can offer—every diminishment of every kind—so that by the grace of God we may be taught his loving lessons and be brought a little nearer to his loving purpose for us and thus be enlarged.

Somehow it's easy to understand the principle of control and denial and loss in the matter of *self*-discipline. It is perfectly plain to anyone who wants to do a difficult and worthwhile thing that he's got to deny himself a thousand unimportant and probably a few hundred important things in order to do the one thing that matters most. Bishop Stephen Neill said that writing is almost entirely a matter of self-discipline. "You must make yourself write." I know. Alas. Sit yourself down, shut yourself up, restrict your enthusiasms, control your maunderings. Think. (Sir Joshua Reynolds wrote, "There is no expedient to which a man will not resort to avoid the real labor of thinking.") Diminishments. Then put things on paper—carefully. Then (and this is the part I resist most strenuously) rewrite. Cut things. Drop things you've spent hours on into the wastebasket.

I lay in bed, luxuriating in the physical bliss, cogitating on the spiritual perplexities. I could not explain why God would restore Lars' lost briefcase and not my New Testament. I could not fathom my friend's suffering or the "waste" of time. But God could. It's got something to do with that great principle of loss being the route to gain, or diminishments being the only way we can finally be enlarged, that is, conformed to the image of Christ.

"Who watched over the birth of the sea?"

The words from God's dialogue with Job came to mind as I listened to the throbbing of the ocean from my bed.

"Have you descended to the springs of the sea, or walked in the unfathomable deep?"

No, Lord, but you have. Nothing in those dark caverns is mysterious to you. Nor is anything in my life or my friend's life. I trust you with the unfathomables.

But you know I'll be back—with the usual question.

— 6 —

Tyrannies and Victories

There are many things people want to be liberated from, many kinds of tyranny from which we would like to escape, but one of the inescapable ones is the tyranny of change. (I didn't make up that idea. I got it from Paul, reading the Phillips' translation of Romans 8:20, 21.)

Most of us are ambivalent about change. We say, "Let's do this for a change," or "I've simply got to have a change," and in the next breath we moan, "Oh dear, how things have changed! They're just not the same anymore." Lots of people do things purely for the sake of doing something different. And one of the ironies (tyrannies are full of ironies) is that things don't necessarily turn out to be all that fresh and original after all.

A group of young intellectuals got together on a farm near Boston and began growing their own fruits and vegetables, milking cows, and building rustic houses in which they could live together simply and study without the distractions of the Establishment. They were fed up with hustle and bustle and just wanted to be themselves. There was a lot of sitting around on floors and stairs, a lot of discussion and reading and dancing under the stars, some trips to Boston for lectures or concerts.

They all had a great interest in Eastern religions, and some of them were followers of a strong-minded woman who thought it was high time members of her sex were liberated and allowed to speak their minds about a few things. Most of the people in this commune believed in nonviolence. Peace was what they were after. They liked long hair and long beards. *Spontaneity* was a great word in their vocabulary and "doing things in crowds" was their idea of the good life.

But the blue the men wore was not jeans. It was tunics. Some wore something called "plain brown holland." The lectures they went to were not on racism but on antislavery. The commune I am talking about was Brook Farm, founded more than a hundred years ago in an effort to find a whole new direction.

I was thinking about that effort, wondering how many times in history it has been repeated, when my aunt happened to give me a box of old family papers. I love old stuff like that and can hardly keep away from it. Here were personal letters from as far back as 1817, old pictures, diaries, house plans, and newspaper clippings. I found myself reading everything, even the advertisements on the backs of the clippings.

A column from *The New York Journal of Commerce*, written by my great-great-uncle and dated July 19, 1864, has this list of things for sale on the back of it: *Common shippers oak timber plank; Sycamore Lumber for Tobacco Boxes; Patent Portable Sectional Houses* (I had just read about modules last week and thought it was quite a change in building technique); *Black Walnut library shelves; Tar—Thick, Thin, and Rope; 150 bbls. Spirits Turpentine in prime shipping order; Cudbear* (I had to look that up—a purple dye made from lichens); *500 bags Singapore pepper; 60 kegs choice Dairy Butter; 75 bales New Orleans Mess* (porridge? I'm not sure); *French and Dutch madder* (the dictionary says a red dye); and a lot of other things like *smoked unbagged hams* (were they better than bagged ones?), *fire crackers, carb ammonia, re-reeled Canton silk,* and *whortleberries.*

It sounded to me like a list of things to do without. But take any similar list from the advertising of today. A magazine that came last week has Oriental porcelain, a lion skin, a $725 crystal koala, and some fifteen-inch potted fig trees. More things I can deny myself.

But there we are again—a lot of effort and study goes on in the advertising business year in and year out. They've improved the presentation of ads, certainly—all those colored pictures (those gorgeous sweeps of lawn, those intimate, elegant living rooms), the catchy, understated text, the catch questions ("Is seepage disturbing your loved ones?")—but they're still up to the same trick, to make me think I ought to feel a need where I felt none.

One entirely predictable thing about life is that there will be changes. Some of the changes are themselves fairly predictable—birth, puberty, marriage, parenthood, suffering, old age, death. We rejoice and recoil when we think about these things. If only there were some safe place where we could halt the progression exactly where we want it.

One morning recently I read in the paper about a prisoner, just released after sixteen years, who asked to remain in prison. He was denied the privilege, so down he went to a tavern, phoned the police to report a robbery, and waited patiently until he was arrested as the thief. Back in his cell he explained that he felt at home there, that he wanted to finish an art course he had started in prison, and that furthermore things had changed a lot in the outside world, and he didn't like it.

I wondered if he saw the cartoon that appeared in *The New Yorker* that same week, showing a guard complaining through the bars to a man in the striped suit, saying, "Take me now. I'll go home on a packed bus, find the wife in tears over some crack a neighbor made, listen to a depressing newscast, bawl the kid out for a lousy report card, eat an underdone casserole, hassle over what TV show we're going to watch, find somebody else has taken the last beer in the icebox and finally settle into a fitful sleep punctured by a neighbor's hi-fi."

The prisoner in the cartoon is slumped down on a bench, hands clasped behind his head, listening to all of this and looking very pleased. People have different ideas of freedom, and they get out of one kind of tyranny and fall into another. The man in the news story wanted the kind of freedom which order, security, and sameness afford. Iron bars didn't bother him as much as change.

I understand that man. I don't like change very much. I am not always moving the furniture around. I don't want any "bright new taste surprises" for breakfast. I want the sofa where it was yesterday and the black coffee just the way I always make it.

It was reassuring to me to learn that C. S. Lewis also liked monotony and routine. Urged time and again to journey abroad to lecture, he stayed home and smoked his pipe and lectured where he felt he belonged. He also wrote wonderful things and remained content with familiar surroundings, able to draw on deep inner resources. Andrew Wyeth found enough to paint in two towns in Pennsylvania and Maine.

The ocean can teach us very many things. Change is its essence. It can be counted on ceaselessly to change, and this is the source of its beauty. The waves roll in, sweep the shore, suck out, and roll in again. It does this in almost the same way each time, but there is something endlessly fascinating in watching how it happens. The swell and the crest, the break and crash, the glass-green turning to milk-white, the cream, the foam, the bubbles, the thin sheet that slides back so smoothly and disappears so suddenly—who can take his eyes off it? But each change is in perfect harmony with the nature of the ocean.

We need not be always seeking something different, something other, out of mere restlessness. There are enough changes we cannot stop, which are of the essence of this life and are meant to be. They are meant to drive us to God.

The world of creation, said Paul, has, in God's purpose, been given hope. "And the hope is that in the end the whole of created life will be rescued from the tyranny of change and decay, and have its share in that magnificent liberty which can only belong to the children of God."

Among the treasures in that box of old family papers was a series of letters from a great-aunt who was serving as a hostess in a rest house in Virginia during World War I. She was a lady unused to working for a living, but her husband dropped dead one day at the bank where he worked, and she had to find a way to support herself. Soldiers and sailors came to the house, some of them terribly homesick, some of them just back from the front with permanent disabilities. The wives and mothers of men who had been killed sometimes arrived at the door in the middle of the night, having just received the sorrowful news. The great-aunt took care of them all.

Her letters to her brother "Chigsie" (Charles Gallaudet Trumbull) are full of cheerfulness and compassion. She was busy helping others every minute of the day and night; as I read her vivid and often humorous accounts of the daily routine, I remember the background of suffering against which she wrote—her own suffering (she could hardly bear to think of returning to the house where she and her husband, Jack, had lived) and that of so many others. But doing everyday duties for the sake of others saved her.

People who have themselves experienced both grief and fear know how alike those two things are. They know the restlessness and loss of appetite, the inability to concentrate, the inner silent wail that cannot be muffled, the feeling of being in a great lonely wilderness which both emotions can produce. They are equally disabling, distracting, and destructive.

One may cry out in prayer and hear no answer. The heavens are brass. One may search Scripture in vain for some word of release and comfort—there are plenty of such words, but how frequently they seem only to mock us, and a voice whispers: "That's not meant for you. You're taking it out of context," and no such word reaches us.

Faith, we know perfectly well, is what we need. We've simply got to exercise faith. But how to do that? How to exercise anything at such a time? "Pull yourself together!" With what? "Cheer up!" How? "Think positively!" But that is a neater trick than we are up to at the moment. We are actually paralyzed. Fear grips us tightly, grief disables us entirely. We have no heart.

At such a time I have been wonderfully calmed and strengthened by doing some simple duty. Nothing valiant or meritorious or spiritual at all—just something that needed to be done, like a bed to be made or a kitchen floor to be washed, one of those things that will never be noticed if you do it, but will most certainly be noticed if you don't. Sometimes it takes everything you have to get up and do it, but it is surprising how strength comes.

Ezekiel was a man who witnessed many strange things and prophesied great cataclysms and splendor. He told us little about himself, but in the twenty-fourth chapter of his book there is a powerful parenthesis:

> The word of the Lord came to me: "Son of man, behold, I am about to take the delight of your eyes away from you at a stroke; yet you shall not mourn or weep nor shall your tears run down. Sigh, but not aloud; make no mourning for the dead. Bind on your turban, and put your shoes on your feet; do not cover your lips nor eat the bread of mourners." So I spoke to the people in the morning, and at evening my wife died. And on the next morning I did as was commanded.

God asked more of Ezekiel than any human being would dare to ask, but he knew his man. He was asking him to "put on a front," to act normally, not as a mourner. To put on turban and shoes and eat his usual food—what extraordinary commands to a man who has just lost the delight of his eyes! But Ezekiel had had plenty of practice in obedience and it was not his habit to bridle. "My wife died . . . I did as I was commanded."

It sounds simple. But not easy. It was heroic, certainly. There are other incidents in the Bible where the doing of very ordinary things helped people out of deep trouble. When Paul was sailing as a prisoner to Italy and was about to be wrecked in the Adriatic Sea, everyone on board was terror-stricken, sailors were trying to escape, the soldiers and centurion and captain were all sure they were doomed and paid little attention to Paul's assurances of faith in God. But when he suggested that they eat and actually took bread himself and gave thanks for it, "then they all were encouraged and ate some food . . . and when they had eaten enough, they lightened the ship, throwing out the wheat into the sea."

Terror had disabled and disoriented them. In their panic they thought only of desperate measures which might have saved a few. But where Paul's faith had had no effect on them, his common sense—"Let's eat"—restored them to their senses. Then they were able to see clearly what the next thing was to be done. From panic came peace. The result was salvation for everybody.

I never noticed until recently that the beautiful story of the woman with the alabaster box of perfume occurs between the high priests' plot to kill Jesus and Judas' deal with them to betray him. The Son of Man knew exactly what he was going to Jerusalem for. But in the face of those tremendous facts he moved with perfect serenity through each day's activities, walking, talking, sleeping, and eating. He even had the grace to sit at supper with his dear friends in Bethany (one of them a leper) and to accept the woman's oblation of love.

He moved on into the Passover with his disciples, taking it as next in order. The Jewish Passover was a feast he had always kept. He would keep it this time, too, as usual. Had we been in his place we would surely have said, "What's the use? Who can go to feast at a time like this?" But our Lord did not halt all activity to brood over what was to come. He was not incapacitated by the fear of suffering, though he well knew that fear. To the question, "What shall I do?" (so often, for us, the cry of despair) he simply answered, "This," and did what lay in his path to do at the moment, trusting himself completely into the hands of his Father. This was how he endured the cross.

We can better imagine the utter paralysis of grief and fear that overcame the disciples of Jesus and the women who loved him in that worst hour when he drooped dead on the cross. No one could think of a thing to do. It was over. God had left. The last shred of hope that God might intervene or that the physician would heal himself had gone. There hung the mutilated corpse, the blood dried by now. But "a good and righteous man" named Joseph from the Jewish town of Arimathea had the presence of mind to think of a few practical things that needed to be done. He went and asked for the body, took it down from the cross, wrapped it in a new linen shroud, and laid it in his own new tomb.

Emmi Bonhoeffer writes in *The Auschwitz Trials*, "From the very moment one feels called to act is born the strength to bear whatever horror one will feel or see. In some inexplicable way, terror loses its overwhelming power when it becomes a task that must be faced."

Joseph's action gave the women the courage and vision they needed to see what they, too, might do. I imagine that the darkest of Friday evenings was made endurable for them because they had work to do for Jesus.

They prepared spices for the body. They rested on Saturday, according to Jewish law, and it was, I believe, a peaceful day for them even while they sorrowed because it held the promise of a clear-cut task next morning. What a morning it turned out to be! But they would have missed it if they had abandoned their common work and given themselves over to grief.

Thomas Carlyle said, "Doubt of any sort cannot be removed except by action." There is wonderful therapy in getting up and doing something. While you are doing, time passes quickly. Time itself will in some measure heal, and "light arises in the darkness," slowly, it seems, but certainly.

According to a poem, the source of which I have been unable to find (can any reader help?), there is a Saxon legend inscribed in an old English parsonage, *Doe the nexte thynge*. "Do it immediately," says the poem, "Do it with prayer, do it reliantly, casting all care." I know it works. I have been hauled out of the Slough of Despond by those four words. And in the doing of whatever comes next, we are shown what to do after that.

7

How to Be Free

Isak Dinesen, the great Danish storyteller, describes two men traveling by dhow to Zanzibar on a full-moon night in 1863. Mira Jama, a much-renowned old man, "the inventions of whose mind have been loved by a hundred tribes," tells a red-haired Englishman "who had been blown about by many winds," that "there are only two courses of thought at all seemly to a person of any intelligence. The one is: What am I to do this next moment?—or tonight, or tomorrow? And the other: What did God mean by creating the world, the sea, and the desert, the horse, the winds, woman, amber, dishes, wine?"

I am captivated by the scene—the warm night, the smooth sea, the creak of the mast, and the quiet voices. But beyond that Mira Jama's statement has for me the ring of truth. It touches the foundation of all that the Bible says to us, for it is a book about man's responsibility and God's purposes. But there is a question which alone is regarded as "relevant" (Mira Jama's word *seemly* is a much better word!) to today's generation, one "up with which I can no longer put," a question discussed in schools, churches, clubs, and "sensitivity groups" ad nauseam. It is WHO AM I? I protest the endless probing and pulse-taking, the anxious inward examination which assumes that the ego is the place to look for answers, and that the truth which makes us free will somehow be found in "knowing oneself." Can we not call it plain old-fashioned selfishness if we ignore the possibility of responsibility to others and to God as the road to freedom? According to Mira Jama, "a person of any intelligence" would want to be informed not of who he is, but of what is expected of him.

One weekend three things happened to my teenage daughter, Valerie, which brought home, more powerfully than any lecture of mine could have done, the tragic delusion of modern youth's quest for identity and freedom. On Friday night her best friend ran away from home. On Saturday night Valerie saw the movie *Easy Rider*. Then on Sunday morning the rector's sermon was on freedom, using *Easy Rider* as an illustration of a misguided pilgrim's progress. Valerie herself saw the relation between these events, and was awed by the "coincidence," to me not less than providential.

Her friend, whom I'll call Becky, had suggested once or twice that she'd like to run away. She had not been happy with her mother, so had decided to try living with her father and stepmother. She didn't like that either. They also expected her to let them know where she was and come home at reasonable hours. This was a bit much for Becky, who had attended a school in New York where "we never had to worry about things like getting homework done or coming to class on time." She filled Val's and other friends' ears with astonishing tales of things she had experienced and took a condescending view of people who were not pot smokers. To her, freedom meant doing what she wanted to do. She had not yet acknowledged to herself that she did not know what she wanted to do. "Maybe the trouble's inside me," she confided to Val. "But I think it's outside. It's my environment. If I can get away from it all, find out who I am, do my own thing . . ."

Easy Rider is the story of two young men who do just that. They use money made in selling dope to cut loose from their responsibilities and head for what looks to them like the Holy City—New Orleans, at Mardi Gras time. One of them starts out by discarding his wristwatch. None of the restrictions of time for him! He is free. And off they go, roaring across the great sunlit spaces of the West, the warm peacefulness of the South. Neither of them notices that if it weren't for the Establishment there would be no smooth highway to travel on, no high-powered bikes to carry them.

The rector's sermon pointed out that true freedom is not to be found in throwing off personal responsibility. The man who runs away from the truth will never be a free man, for it is the truth alone, sought within the circle of his commitments, which will make him free.

Dietrich Bonhoeffer, a man who epitomized true freedom in his acceptance, for God's sake, of the prison cell and death, wrote: "If you set out to seek freedom, then learn above all things to govern your soul and your senses. . . . Only through discipline may a man learn to be free."

Freedom and discipline have come to be regarded as mutually exclusive, when in fact freedom is not at all the opposite, but the final reward, of discipline. It is to be bought with a high price, not merely claimed. The world thrills to watch the grace of Peggy Fleming on the ice, or the marvelously controlled speed and strength of a racehorse. But the skater and horse are free to perform as they do only because they have been subjected to countless hours of grueling work, rigidly prescribed, faithfully carried out. Men are free to soar into space because they have willingly confined themselves in a tiny capsule designed and produced by highly trained scientists and craftsmen, have meticulously followed instructions and submitted themselves to rules which others defined.

I spent some time living with a jungle tribe whose style of life looked enviably "free." They wore no clothes, lived in houses without walls, had no idea whatever of authority, paid no taxes, read no books, took no vacations. But they had a well-defined goal. They wanted to stay alive. It was as simple as that. And in a jungle, which can look very hostile indeed to one not accustomed to living there, they had learned to live. They accepted with grace and humor the awful weather, the gnats, the mud, thorns, snakes, steep hills, and deep forests which made their lives difficult. They never even spoke of "roughing it." They didn't know anything else. They'd walk for hours with hundred-pound baskets on their backs and when they reached their destination, perhaps in a tropical downpour, they did not so much as say, "Whew!" They knew what was expected of them and did it as a matter of course. None asked, "Who am I?" They asked only, "What am I to do this next moment?" If it were to hunt or to make poison for darts, a man did that, or if it were to go out and clear new planting space, a woman did that. Their freedom to live in that jungle depended on a well-defined goal and on their willingness to discipline themselves in order to reach it. No one could "give" them this freedom.

I lived with these footloose people in their "jungle" environment—a nonproductive member of their community—and enjoyed a kind of freedom which even hippies might envy. But I was free only because the Indians worked. My freedom was contingent upon their acceptance of me as a liability and, incidentally, upon my own willingness to confine myself to a forest clearing where all I heard was a foreign language.

So we come back to Mira Jama and Becky and the "Easy Riders," and their search for meaning in life. It can be found only in God's purpose, I believe, in what he originally meant when he made us. "If you are faithful to what I have said, you are truly my disciples [those who are being disciplined]," Jesus said. "And you will know the truth and the truth will set you free."

8

All That Was Ever Ours

In his beautiful book *For the Life of the World*, Alexander Schmemann says that time is

> the first "object" of our Christian faith and action. Through time on the one hand we experience life as a possibility, growth, fulfillment, as a movement toward the future. Through time, on the other hand, all future is dissolved in death and annihilation. . . . By itself time is nothing but a line of telegraph poles strung out into the distance and at some point along the way is our death.

All my life I have been acutely conscious of time, having grown up in a family where six o'clock meant five fifty-five, and because my father was superintendent of the Sunday school we got there as much as an hour early. In the past ten or fifteen years I have become more conscious of it, not only for the obvious reason that when one reaches middle age he knows it's running out, but also because as a speaker I'm used to being told how much time I'm allowed (ten minutes, thirty minutes) and I try to stick to it. (I am agonizingly aware of time when the speaker who precedes me is cheerfully unaware of it.) I marvel at the program planners who arrange to have, following an hour and a half of banqueting, a "short" business meeting, a "few" acknowledgments (getting the ladies out of the kitchen for a round of applause always takes a long time—one of them is still wiping her hands on an apron and won't come, another only peeks around the door with the sheepish protest, "But I didn't do anything!"), a couple of guitar numbers (is there a short guitar number?), a testimony or two, and one of those things we used to call movies which are now, for reasons beyond my understanding, called "multimedia presentations," before the speaker or speakers take the platform. Time doesn't seem to mean much of anything to those planners until the speaker stands up and then they wonder how in the world it got so late and hope most fervently that the speaker will make it short.

But if time is the first object of our faith and actions as Christians, we need to learn to redeem it, to say with the psalmist, "My times are in Thy hands," and to realize that it has been once for all transformed. God incarnate entered time. Jesus Christ "suffered under Pontius Pilate," a particular Roman procurator in a particular place at a particular point in history, redeeming us and the world we live in, transforming forever that bleak "line of telegraph poles strung out into the distance." Nothing is meaningless. Nothing, for the Christian, is a dead end. All endings are beginnings.

I need to remember this just now, because the Cottage is about to go on the market. "The Cottage" is a summer place in the White Mountains of New Hampshire, built in 1889 by my great-great uncle and aunt, and the scene of gloriously happy family vacations ever since. It was to me as a child the very vestibule of heaven. We would leave Philadelphia on the night Pullman, the "Bar Harbor Express," and I remember the delirium of joy with which I settled into the berth, my clothes safely stowed in the little hammock, and fell asleep, to be awakened in New Haven by the shifting of the cars as the train was divided into different sections. I would lift the blind and see the brakeman passing with his lantern, watch the baggage trucks rolling by, and try to read in the dim light the thrillingly romantic names on the freight cars in the yards—"Seaboard Airline," "Lackawanna," "Chicago and Northwestern," "Route of the Phoebe Snow," "Atchison, Topeka, and Santa Fe." I remember the jerking of the uncoupling and the satisfying crunch of the coupling, the loud hissing of steam and then the gentle rolling out of the station, the giant engine building up speed until the clickety-click reached the rhythm that once again put me to sleep.

In the morning I woke to see the Connecticut River valley, and it was not long before we pulled into Littleton, where we were met by my grandfather's Buick and driven the eight miles to the Cottage. My stomach tightened with the joy of that first glimpse of the two brick chimneys, visible as we crossed the Gale River Bridge, and then, as we turned up the driveway, I could see the beloved house, the breakfast table set in the sun on the front quarter of the porch. (The porch ran all the way around the house, which was rectangular, built stockade-style, with six-inch spruce blocks for walls in the lower portion, shingles above.)

The sound of footsteps hurrying from the kitchen on the old boards. The creak of the hinges on the massive door which had a key eight inches long. (It was said that Uncle Will had the big iron lock and key before he built the house and had to construct a door on a comparable scale.) A race around the porch to see if the little cart we played with was still in its place, to look into the separate cabin which was the kitchen at the back of the porch, a pause to look at the mountains—Lafayette, Artists' Bluff, Bald, Cannon, Kinsman—blue against the sky, always dependably the same, strong, comforting ("So the Lord is round about them that fear Him"), waiting for us to climb them once more. In the living room, the huge fireplace with its three-foot andirons; the green china clock on the mantel, the guns in their niche; the fishing rods cradled in bentwood hooks suspended from the ceiling; the Texas Longhorns, the deer head; the portrait of Uncle Will on the wall; the rocking chairs where Grandpa and Grandma Howard always sat by the heavy writing table which Uncle Will had made with his own hands; the converted kerosene lamps; the little melodion which we used for accompaniment at our Sunday-evening hymn sings (the "natives" came to these, including a little old lady who claimed she couldn't sing "half's good's a crow"); the cushioned settee with a lid which lifted to reveal a furry mechanical bear, a black lace parasol, a music box, and a mummified human child's foot, brought from some ancient tomb in Egypt by Uncle Will back when he was scrounging the world for things to put in the then new Metropolitan Museum in New York.

In the back parlor were crumbling leather-bound books, a set of bells, a stereopticon with magic pictures of ice caves and frozen waterfalls, astonishing in the perfection and depth of each gleaming crystal, the glass cases of moths and butterflies which Aunt Annie had lured by stretching a bedsheet in the light of a lantern on the porch at night. And upstairs were books and more books, brightly colored stuffed birds from foreign lands, Aunt Annie's flower press, a vial of attar of roses from a forgotten tomb, and life-sized paintings of improbably large brook trout that Uncle Will had caught, painted, and pasted to the door panels. There was the little room with the bird's-eye maple-andbamboo furniture where I slept, snuggling down under a feather quilt and listening to the wind in the white pines, the sound of the river flowing over the stones, and there was a poem tacked to the wall: "Sleep sweetly in this quiet room, O thou, whoe'er thou art."

And oh, the smell of the place! Year after year it was the same. Year after year we rushed in and breathed that sweetness—old wood, old leather, old books, the perfume of pine and balsam and wood smoke. There is no accounting for that fragrance, but it is still there, still the same, intoxicating to us who know it, still redolent of all the years of happiness, and now someone else will breathe it, someone who doesn't know its meaning at all.

How shall we say good-bye to the glory of that house, how accept the sadness that it is no longer ours? By making it, as Schmemann says, of time, the object of our Christian faith and action. By recognizing that time has two dimensions—it brings things to an end, and it gives us always new beginnings. Christ is the Alpha and the Omega, the beginning and the end, and we bring to him all of our beginnings and endings, all the hope and sadness that they cause us, all of the work done and the pleasures enjoyed as well as all our plans for work to be done and pleasures to be enjoyed.

> So, through life, death, through sorrow, and through sinning,
> He shall suffice me, for He hath sufficed.
> Christ is the End, for Christ was the Beginning,
> Christ the Beginning, for the End is Christ.
>
> F. W. H. Meyer
> *St. Paul*

We give thanks, then, as we bring these things to him, and in the giving of thanks we signal our total acceptance of his will for us.

We are also granted temporary reprieves. Aunt Clara called the other night to say that it's not going on the market after all. Not exactly, anyway. She has figured out some kind of plan which may make the place available to family members for a little while longer.

There is a storybook sort of attic in the Cottage, with two bedrooms built into it originally as servants' rooms. As our family expanded I slept in one of these instead of in the bedroom on the second floor with the bird's-eye maple-and-bamboo furniture. This room had an old-fashioned bed, bureau, and wooden washstand on which stood a great brown-and-white china basin, a soap dish to match, and two pitchers, large and small. Inside the little door that opened at the bottom of the washstand was a matching chamber pot. The most interesting feature of this room, however, was what my aunt called her rogues' gallery, a long row of black-and-white photographs of her female college classmates, all with demure waves dipping low over the forehead, all with the peculiarly ill-fitting blouses of the thirties, all with the same bland and trustful expression, gazing mildly down at me as I lay in the bed. My aunt called them girls. To me they were most certainly not girls. They had been to college, they were old, they were unknown and unapproachable, and the unrelieved sameness of hairdo, expression, and costume created in my mind a distant strange world of which I would never be a part.

Under the attic eaves were other things which had the same effect. There was a small trunk of the variety made to fit nicely on the top of a stagecoach. This had belonged to great-great Aunt Annie of (I knew from her photographs) rigid posture, black silk dresses, and only the faintest hint of a smile. There were also woodcuts depicting Adam and Eve confronting Satan, or angels and cherubim and stallions and obese ladies in impossible positions. These had been relegated to the attic, probably by my mother, "because they gave the children nightmares," but I suspected it was because every one of them portrayed one or more beings, celestial or terrestrial, who in her opinion were not adequately clothed. These my brothers and I crawled into the dusty recesses to study at our leisure. To this day Satan appears in my imagination with the same fierce and wicked face of those woodcuts, although I have managed to improve on the images of Adam and Eve.

The tiny brown field mice with delicate pink feet which ran up and down the electric wires and scattered seeds among the picture frames and mattresses of the attic were my friends. I would lie on my stomach holding my breath, not moving an eyelash, waiting for them to appear at their holes in the floorboards. I felt with them a special kinship in that we were the living denizens of this attic—intruders, perhaps, but here and alive, in spite of Satan and the cherubs, the great-great aunt, and the college "girls" who were here long before we came.

There was a lovely pine grove behind the Cottage with a path that ran through it to what Aunt Annie had named "The Meeting of the Waters," junction of two clear mountain streams, Gale River and Pond Brook. Wooden seats had been constructed encircling several of the larger pine trees, and when I was very small my grandfather took me to sit on one of them while he showed me how to build a house of twigs on the floor of the forest.

My aunt taught me the wild flowers that grew near the Cottage, and I pressed them in a brown dime-store notebook—cinquefoil, Quaker lady, and twin flower from the pine woods, wild orchid and lady's slipper from the low, grassy place at the river's level, devil's paintbrush, butter-and-eggs, goldenrod, and Queen Anne's lace from the meadow in front of the Cottage. Years later I learned the bracken, ferns, and mosses, and showed other small children the wonders of the hairy cap moss—how you take off its hairy cap, lift the lid of the tiny "salt shaker," and pour out its pale green powder into the palm of your hand.

There were our fields, our own woods, our swimming place down at the Meeting of the Waters. The very rocks belonged, we felt, to us. In the field were three large granite rocks, too heavy to move when the rest were cleared for planting long before. My brothers and I each claimed one of these as our own. We would go out and "ride" them, imagining ourselves mounted on an elephant, a camel, and a tortoise. There was "The Big Rock," a gigantic boulder in the middle of Gale River with a deep pool beside it to swim in. Occasionally there was a trout and often we caught the bigger fish we always called suckers. The rock had a beautiful flat top where you could toast yourself after coming out of the frigid water, feeling the warmth of the sun on one side of you and the warmth of the rock on the other.

All of this, then, was ours—even the intoxicating smell of the cold brooks running over the clean stones between the sun-warmed pine and spruce-covered banks. The land on the far side of Pond Brook belonged, in my mind, to God. It was wilderness. There were no trails but animal trails there, and we felt that there were deer and maybe now and then a bear.

We grew up in the Depression, and although we had no idea we were poor, we had little idea how rich we were in things other than money. That Cottage was one of the great riches, with its treasures inside and its priceless scenery outside, its inexhaustible supply of things to do, things to look at and smell and revel in, the mountains to climb and the woods to explore, the streams to bathe in, the rocks to own.

When I go back there now there is, mingled with the smell of spruce, the smell of char-broiled steaks floating across meadow and stream. There's a campground now in God's own wilderness. If ever the deer and the bear were really there as we hoped, they are gone, replaced by campers, tents, trailers, and displaced people on that inevitably fruitless quest for what isn't there. They don't listen to the wind in the trees or the brooks flowing over rocks. They've got the transistor radio on full volume while they set up the outdoor grill. They don't lie in the dark and look at the moon over Lafayette—they've just pumped up the pressure lantern or switched on the lights that have by this time, for all I know, been wired in across the brook. They wade into our stream and climb over the Big Rock and toss their beer cans down where the suckers used to be.

I have to get a firm grip on myself and remember that none of this deprives me of what I had. "All that was ever ours," wrote Amy Carmichael of India, "is ours forever." That wonderful place was one of the stations of my life. It helped to shape my tastes and loves and imagination and vision of God, and I remember his command to the people of Israel: "Thou shalt remember all the way which the Lord thy God led thee."

They were to remember all of it. Most of it, I suppose, was more boring than memorable on that desert journey, and they had to go from Point A to Point B to Point C and all the way to Point Z in obedience, whether or not anything interesting happened along the way. But there were special places where God met them in special ways, and thus he helped them to review his leading. He knew how their memory would need jogging. The Cottage is one of the stations I go back to in my memory with joy. There are, of course, other kinds of places as well, places not at all like the Cottage which I would as soon forget. But, as Phillips Brooks prayed, I pray, "O Lord, by all Thy dealings with us, whether of light or darkness, of joy or pain, let us be brought to Thee." It is he to whom and with whom we travel, and while he is the End of our journey, he is also at every stopping place.

9

Truth Telling

I built a house in New Hampshire a few years ago. The bulldozing for the foundation had barely begun when a shiny car drove up and out stepped a man dressed in very clean work clothes. He took off his hard hat and introduced himself as "the best gosh-dam well-driller in the whole North Country." I needed a well, and he drilled it and did a good job. After that he would drop by whenever he had work in the neighborhood. The coffee I gave him was a small price to pay to hear him talk. He held opinions about everything and was afraid of nothing and nobody. And he certainly knew how to tell a story. I listened enthralled. He had his own way of running a business ("We need your business—our business is going in the hole" was his motto, painted on the side of his drilling rigs) and his own code of ethics, both of which worked fine for him.

"I've worked for people, and I'm not lying to you," he said one day. "You can call my wife right up and she'll go over the checkbook, and I'll bet you over the last five years there's been fifteen people I've gone and drilled a well for and give 'em two percent off if they pay in ten days. Well, like the money'd be coming from the bank or something and it might go thirty days and the people were honest, they wouldn't take their two percent and I'd send it back. Now how many guys will send back money once they get it? Like, it'd be a two-thousand-dollar job and that'd be, what, forty dollars? Yeah. You can ask my wife and she'll show you the checkbook. Because I just don't do things that way, I mean that, life's too short.

"Now let's say you're in business. You're doin' something so let's say I go and say, 'Well, heck, don't hire Betty Elliot, she don't know what she's doin'.' Well, all right, they may go and hire you anyway and you may do the best job in the world. Now isn't that gonna make me look stupid? Sometimes I go to look at a job and a guy'll say to me he can get somebody else to drill his well for six dollars a foot when I'm asking seven. I'll say to him, 'You know I didn't come up here to give you an education about my competition, I never give 'em a thought. All I know is I know what I'm doin' and I've got something to show for it. If you need this well drilled I can drill it. As far as I'm concerned half my competition stinks, but if you want to ask me to come here to see you about a well I'm not comin' here to run down my competition because the idea of it is you might hire one of my competitors and he might do a wonderful job and then you can say, "Well, I don't know what on earth he was shootin' off his mouth about."' I can't see that kind of business, can you? Life's too short.

"But the way I look at life is that no matter who it is—so long as they're somewheres near square everybody's gotta get a living. I mean I'm not planning to drill all the wells, but so what if I don't? I do what I can, and I do it good. The other guy's gotta eat, he's got a wife and kids, too, so what's the difference?

"I never charge anything for setting up the rig, either. A lot of guys, they want three hundred dollars for setting up and they want their money the day they're done drillin', but then if you got to put the pump in and there's something wrong, well, what're you gonna do? You've had it, and you've got to stop payment on a check, you gotta work fast. But I don't do things that way. I'm not interested in it. But you've gotta go out there and do something and life is short. If you gotta be crooked on everything you do and you can't look people in the face, you know full well they think you're a crook and it's a pretty short world to be doin' that all the time, I would say."

It is a short world, and it doesn't take more brains than most of us have to figure out that honesty is a good thing if it helps business and keeps us from looking too stupid. It's the best policy, obviously, but it isn't usually much more than that. It's one of those things, along with eating and dieting, taxation, religion, and loving your neighbor, that we all feel can be carried too far. Too far, that is, if the matter concerns ourselves.

"The people in your organization are certainly the most honest bunch I've ever seen," a woman said to a friend of mine.

"Honest? How do you mean?"

"Well, honest about each other."

We can stand a lot of honesty that concerns other people, and we jump to the defense of protesters so long as they're protesting things for which we're not directly responsible. But we are marvelously uncritical and generous when it comes right down to the nitty-gritty of our private lives. You won't catch us carrying things to extremes there.

People do overeat, but it hasn't been my problem. Dieting, on the other hand, can be carried too far and that piece of pie does look delicious. As for religion, a good thing, of course—an excellent thing if you don't get too much of it at once. And I'm willing to pay my taxes. I understand that the country can't run without them, but this bill, now. . . . Loving my neighbor? I do. But how far do you think a person ought to be expected to go anyhow?

At a camp where my husband worked for several summers the counselors had to grade each camper on certain character traits. Was he, for example, exceptionally, moderately, or fairly honest?

A man in Elmhurst, Illinois, found two Brinks money bags containing $183,000. He threw them, unopened, into the trunk of his car and for four days wondered what to do with them. (He mentioned later that he did not even think to tell his wife. I think she would have known what to do.)

"I didn't know it was money," he told newsmen. "I thought it might be mail. I forgot about them until I began reading stories in the paper. Then I realized what I had. I had always daydreamed about finding a lot of money, but it became a reality and things changed. I had to call."

Asked why he didn't break the seals on the bags he said, "You don't break seals on people's parcels. That would muddle things considerably. I'm an honest man within reasonable limits."

The Brinks company awarded him $18,000 for his honesty, which raises the question of whether his was, in fact, a "reasonable" honesty, for if he had been dishonest he might possibly have succeeded in keeping the $183,000 for himself, along with, at the very least, some sleepless nights.

It is a short world, and if this is the only world, we can play it like a game—fair and somewhere near square. That ought to be good enough, and a man ought to be allowed to get what he's willing to pay for.

But what about gaining the whole world and losing your own soul? Those words apply to another world altogether, the long one, where the rules are not the same at all, where things like poverty and meekness and sorrow and hunger and purity of heart lead to happiness. Then, too, the Rule Book has things about living "honestly in all things," "providing for honest things, not only in the sight of the Lord, but also in the sight of men," and (who can stand up to this one?) about the Lord's desiring "truth in the inward parts." It is what I would have to call an unreasonable honesty, beyond any of us, and we have to call out, "Lord, save me!" And that is what he does.

Recently I met a friend for lunch whom I had not seen for twenty years. As I approached the restaurant I was thinking the usual thoughts: *Will she have changed much? Will I recognize her? Will we be able to find things to talk about?*

I saw her as soon as I got there, and I knew that if I said, "Why, Helen, you haven't changed a bit!" it would be a bald lie. The truth was that Helen was beautiful now. She had never been a beauty in college. The years and her experiences (some of them of a kind of suffering I knew nothing about) had given her a deep womanliness, a kind of tender strength. Her eyes glowed, there was passion about her mouth, and the lines of her face revealed a strength of character she could not have had when she was a college student. So, instead of the usual pleasantries, I simply started with the truth. I told her what I saw in her face. Of course she was taken aback, but I am sure that this unorthodox beginning did not render further conversation more difficult. We were able to get down to the real things in life, things that matter and that had changed us both, rather than spending an hour on the ages of our children, their mates and careers, and our latest diets and recipes.

We all know that the truth often hurts. We use this cliché as a defense for having hurt someone, and sometimes it is indeed necessary to tell this kind of truth. But there is truth which does not hurt—truth which encourages and surprises with delight and gratitude. What if a teacher sees that a colleague of hers has succeeded in breaking down the resistance of a pupil who has been the despair of the other teachers, the talk of the faculty lunchroom? The change in the student is noticed, a sigh of relief is heaved, but who goes to the teacher herself and says,

"Thanks! You've done what the rest of us couldn't do!" How many are free enough from themselves to recognize the worth of others and to speak of it honestly?

A lady who is a good many years older than I tells me often of the aunt who was a mother to her throughout her childhood. "Auntie" impressed her with the need to tell the truth—the welcome kind—and she would add emphatically, "Tell them now." My friend calls me on the telephone—sometimes to thank me for a note or a little gift, sometimes to tell me what my friendship means to her.

"You remember what Auntie always said," she will say, "so, I'm telling you now." There would be no way for me to exaggerate how she has cheered and helped me.

I was talking with a lady who had been a missionary for forty years, and I noticed that she had exceptionally lovely hands. "Has anyone ever told you your hands are beautiful?" I asked. The dear soul was so flustered one might have thought I had committed an indecency. She looked at her hands in amazement.

"Why . . . why no. I don't think anyone ever has!" But she saw that I meant it, and she had the grace to hear the truth. She said thank you.

"Tell it like it is," is the watchword today. But suppose it's lovely? Suppose it's actually beautiful? C. S. Lewis said that the most fatal of all nonconductors is embarrassment. It seems to me that life is all too short to let embarrassment deprive us and our friends of the pleasure of telling the happy truth. Suppose the boy who does your lawn does it fast, trims it perfectly, and takes care of the tools? Suppose the clerk who waits on you happens to be the most gracious one you've ever encountered? Suppose even that your husband—when you stop for once to look at him, to think about him as a person and as a man—seems to you to be the best man you know?

Tell them.

Tell them now.

10

In a Hospital Waiting Room

I have been a patient in a hospital only once, when I was six years old and had my tonsils out. But during my husband's last illness I saw what that life was like. If you are in terrible pain or have broken an arm or leg, the huge gray cluster of buildings can look like heaven, for inside are people who can do wonderful things to help. For a woman about to have a baby the hospital is full of anticipation and happiness. But for those who do not know what their disease may be, or who have been told that it is, finally, just what they most dreaded, the experience of going to the hospital can be an overpowering one of terror and horror and helplessness.

If one arrives in such a state, who can describe the effect of walking through the big glass doors into the bustling lobby of a city hospital where some rush around with many things to do and some wait? Nurses, doctors, visitors, and ambulance drivers come and go. Others sit silently, some in wheelchairs (the ever-patient patients), waiting for someone, waiting to be taken somewhere, waiting for some dreaded or hoped-for word.

As we came through the doors a young man came toward us, using a new pair of crutches with the one leg left to him. A middle-aged couple wheeled a grown-up handicapped son toward a waiting taxi. A stretcher with a blanketed form on it was brought in from a police ambulance. A very tall black youth carried two potted plants done up in rustling green paper.

People stood at the reception desk waiting to ask where to find a patient or a department or a doctor. The harried receptionist hardly looked at the questioners, giving out her short, practiced replies as though she had been affronted. We joined the line, got directions for the radiation department, and took the elevator to the fifth floor, where we were told to follow the blue painted line on the hall floor. A boy who looked too young to be an orderly was pushing a wheelchair down the hall. A gray-haired lady sat in the chair weeping. Another boy raced around the corner, clipped the young orderly on the shoulder, and the two exchanged some unintelligible banter behind the weeping woman's back.

We found the waiting room for the radiation department. It was nearly full, but we hung up our coats and found places to sit. I was in that state of exquisite sensitivity described so well in the Psalms in words such as these: "I am poured out like water, and all my bones are out of joint; my heart is like wax, it is melted within my breast; my strength is dried up like a potsherd, and my tongue cleaves to my jaws; thou dost lay me in the dust of the earth." Water, wax, broken pots, dust. Not much to fortify us there. "Lord, have mercy on us," I said (not aloud), "Christ, have mercy on us."

It was a winter afternoon and grew dark early. The only window in the room looked out on a gray brick wall.

A man with a large swelling on his neck, outlined in red ink, came in and put on his coat and left, his treatment over for that day. Then a little boy arrived with his mother. He had a red square with an X in it painted on each temple. Christ, have mercy on us. How can we endure?

The mother and son took off their coats, the mother sat down, but the boy was rambunctious and found things to do—messing up magazines, tipping over an ashtray, blowing out the match as his mother tried to light a cigarette.

Husbands and wives sat talking quietly and, I noticed, always kindly. One couple caught my attention particularly. They were shabbily dressed, and the man was badly crippled. It was the wife, however, who was there for radiation. I watched them talk to each other. They had courage, and they were quite evidently in love. Those who had been there before had become a fellowship. They waved, smiled, greeted each other. How could they? How did they manage to carry on in so normal a fashion?

Almost imperceptibly the picture began to take on a new color for me. An older lady in a pale green uniform came into the room, smiled at all of us, and asked if anyone would like coffee or ginger ale. I will always remember what that smile did for me, and the gracious, simple way in which she handed the beverages.

The nurse who came to call the patients for their treatments had a smile, too, and a cheerful voice (but not the forced cheerfulness of which nurses are so often accused). As she walked out of the waiting room with a patient, she put her arm around him. That touch (I wonder if she will ever know this?) was redemptive.

We had a long wait and I tried to read, but I kept looking up and watching what was going on in that crowded little room. The lady with the coffee I saw as our hostess, and I thought of the word *graciousness*, the highest compliment paid to a hostess. What she does comes out of what she is herself, but she forgets herself completely. Her only thought is the comfort and ease of her guests. This lady was, I suppose, a volunteer. She gave herself and her time and expected nothing in return, but she smiled and brought to that dark place an unexpected shining.

An old man waiting for his treatment called the rambunctious little boy over and began to do tricks with pennies for him. Soon the mother was smiling, others were watching as the boy's face lit up with surprise and delight.

It came to me then that what made that room shine was the action of grace. "If I make my bed in hell," wrote the psalmist, "behold, Thou art there." That hospital had seemed to me the vestibule of hell an hour earlier. But behold, God was there—in the lady in green, in the nurse who by her touch brought comfort and courage, in the couple whose love showed through, in the man doing tricks.

Grace is a marvelous but elusive word. "Unmerited favor" is the definition most of us know. It means self-giving, too, and springs from the person's own being without condition or consideration of whether the object is deserving. Grace may be unnoticed. But there are usually some who will notice. "Where sin abounded, grace did much more abound," wrote St. Paul. And those who are in a desperation of suffering will notice it, will notice even its lightest touch, and will hold it a precious, an incalculably valuable thing.

— 11 —

Boredom

In the book *A Sort of Life* Graham Greene tells how he has struggled, ever since he was very young, to fend off boredom. He once had a dentist extract ("but with ether") a perfectly good tooth for no better reason than that he was bored and this seemed like an interesting diversion. He tried several times to commit suicide and six times played Russian roulette, using a revolver with six chambers—a dangerous game, but not, heaven help us, boring.

Dorothy Parker was famous for her wit before she was thirty. She had great charm, a fine education, a fascinating kind of beauty, and many interesting friends. But she was utterly bored. She, too, thought of suicide, and was quoted in John Keats' book *You Might As Well Live* as saying:

> Razors pain you;
> Rivers are damp;
> Acids stain you;
> And drugs cause cramp.
> Guns aren't lawful;
> Nooses give;

> Gas smells awful;
> You might as well live.

Her life story seemed to me the exact illustration of acedia, or accidie, which is an old word for boredom, but a word that includes depression, sloth, irritability, lazy languor, and bitterness. "This rotten sin," wrote Chaucer, "maketh a man heavy, wrathful and raw." Poor Miss Parker had been so irritable and raw with people—she had treated even her friends unspeakably badly—that she spent her last years alone in a hotel in New York, her pitiful, neglected dogs and her liquor bottles almost her only companions.

Gertrude Behanna says, on her record, "God Isn't Dead," that she has come to believe that it is a real sin to bore people. When we stop to think about it, most of us would readily agree. But how many of us have thought of boredom itself, so long as it affects only ourselves, as a sin? The Bible speaks of joy as a Christian virtue. It is one of the fruits of the Spirit, and often we find that it characterizes the people of God whose stories we read in the Bible. The worship of God in the Old Testament was accompanied by the most hilarious demonstrations of gladness—dancing, shouting, and music-making. (This was to me one of the most impressive features of life in modern Israel when I visited there.)

Joy is not a word we use much nowadays. We think of it poetically as the opposite of sorrow, another word that does not often come into conversation. Both words represent experiences one does not normally have every day.

But I think we are mistaken. I think joy is meant to be an everyday experience, and as such it is the exact opposite of boredom, which seems to be the everyday experience (am I being overly pessimistic?) of most Americans. I get the impression that everybody is always hoping for a chance to get away from it all, relax, unwind, get out of these four walls, find somewhere, somehow, some action or excitement. Advertising, of course, has done a splendid job of creating in us greed for things we would never have thought of wanting, and thereby convincing us that whatever we have is intolerably boring. Attributing human wants to animals, we easily swallow the TV commercials that tell us that Morris the cat doesn't want tuna fish every day, he wants eight different flavors.

"Godliness with contentment is great gain." Those words were written a long time ago to a young man by an older man who had experienced almost the gamut of human suffering, including being chained day and night to a prison guard. Contentment is another word which has fallen into disuse. We think of it, perhaps, in connection with cows—the best milk comes from contented ones, doesn't it?—but it doesn't take much to content a cow. Peace and fodder are probably all it asks. We are not cows. What does it take to content us? How could Paul, after what he had been through, write as he did to Timothy?

C. S. Lewis, one of the most godly and civilized men I have ever heard of, exemplified what Paul was getting at. Lewis wrote that he was never bored by routine. In fact, he said, he liked it. He had what his anthologist Clyde S. Kilby called "a mind awake." Why should routine spoil it? Pictures of him show a joyful man. But he was not a man unacquainted with poverty, hard work, and suffering any more than Paul was. He knew them, but he knew, too, what lay beyond. "All joy," he wrote to a friend, "(as distinct from mere pleasure, still more amusement) emphasizes our pilgrim status; always reminds, beckons, awakens desire. Our best havings are wantings."

Those wantings lie in the deepest places of our being, and they are for the kind of joy that, according to Lewis, is "the serious business of heaven." So we waste our time, our money, and our energies when we pursue so frantically the pleasures which we hope will bring us relief from boredom. We end up bored with everything and everybody. Work which can be joyful if accepted as a part of the eternal order and a means to serve, becomes only drudgery. Our pettiest difficulties, not to mention our big ones, are cause for nothing but complaint and self-pity. All circumstances not deliberately arranged by us look like obstacles to be rid of. We consume much and produce little; we get depressed, and depression is actually dangerous and destructive.

But there is another way. Paul made it perfectly clear that his contentment had nothing to do with how desirable his circumstances were. "I am content with weaknesses, insults, hardships, persecutions and calamities." It is no list of amusements. How, then, did it work? It worked by a mysterious transforming power, something that reversed things like weakness and hardship, making them into strength and joy. Is there any chance that it will work for us? Is there for us, too, an antidote for boredom? The promise of Christ was not for Paul alone. "My grace is sufficient for you." It's a gift to be accepted. If we refuse it, nothing will be enough and boredom will be the story of our lives.

— 12 —

Some of My Best Friends Are Books

I have almost always been surrounded by books. I wouldn't be surprised if my mother put some in the crib along with my toys, just to get me used to them early. The first house I remember living in was one of those double ones of which there are hundreds in the suburbs of Philadelphia. We lived in Germantown, in what was probably a cramped house (although to me as a child it seemed large) and there were books in the living room, books in the dining room, books in all of the bedrooms and tall bookcases lining the halls. My father came home at night with a briefcase full of papers and books.

Before I could read much myself I looked at picture books, like everybody else. I remember the lovely women and elegantly handsome men in Charles Dana Gibson's book of drawings. I went back again and again to an animal book which had a horrifyingly hideous photo of an angry gorilla with teeth bared. The beautiful little pictures in Beatrix Potter's books of neatly furred small animals gave me a delicious feeling of order and comfort. My mother read these aloud to me, and how eagerly I stooped with Lucie to enter Mrs. Tiggywinkle's laundry; or accompanied Simpkin the cat as he made his way through Gloucester's snowy lanes. Mr. MacGregor was a big, bad bogeyman to me. Mother read, too, the Christopher Robin stories, and I found myself identifying her with Kanga, my older brother Phil with Pooh, Dave with Piglet, and myself, alas but inescapably, with Eeyore.

Evenings at home were often spent with the whole family sitting together, each with his head in a book. Or at times my father would read aloud. He bored us to death reading passages from Jonathan Edwards, George Whitefield, or George Borrow. *The Bible in Spain* was "good writing," he said, and he wanted us to hear it. He loved good writing, and as an editor had to read an awful lot of appallingly bad writing, but I am grateful now for his efforts to teach us the difference. He also read sometimes to us from Henry A. Shute's *Real Diary of a Real Boy*, which got the closest thing to a belly laugh I ever heard out of my sedate father.

A big dictionary was always within reach of the dining room table because it was there that arguments most frequently arose over words. He wanted them quickly settled and made us look up the words in question.

A part of each summer was spent at "The Cottage," a big old lodge-type house in the White Mountains built by my great-great uncle, who was, among other things, editor of the *New York Journal of Commerce* and a writer of books. His bedroom on the second floor, an enormous paneled one with a huge fireplace, had hardly been rearranged at all since he died, and one wall was still lined with crumbling leather-bound books. A rainy day in the mountains was a chance for me to pore over field manuals from the Civil War, great volumes on law, Mrs. Oliphant's novels, or a tiny set, tinnily printed, of the unabridged *Arabian Nights*.

There were magazines on the bottom shelves, too—old ones, with advertisements of Pear's soap or Glen kitchen ranges, and I found in them serialized stories by Robert Louis Stevenson.

The first full-length book I recall reading was not a piece of great literature, but it had a great effect on my malleable mind. It was called *Hell on Ice*, the saga of sixty men who attempted to reach the North Pole by way of the Bering Strait. Only a few survived, and I agonized with them as they froze and starved on the icy wastes. I was carried out of myself and my pleasant porch hammock into danger, suffering, and death. I became aware of vulnerability, mortality, and human courage.

To my detriment I managed to go through four years of high school without reading more than two or three classics. I had a good freshman English teacher who made me see vividly the world of chivalry and heraldry through *Ivanhoe*, so that I still love to visit the medieval halls of museums. In my junior or senior year I very hastily skimmed *David Copperfield* in order to write a book report. I may have read one or two others which I have entirely forgotten, but literature was merely a requirement. No other teacher made me understand what it was all about. (B. F. Westcott said, "It is the office of art to reveal the meaning of that which is the object of sense.")

But of course there was the Bible, in a class all by itself. This was The Book in our home, and we heard it read every day, usually twice a day. The King James English was as simple and familiar to me, with all its "beholds" and "it came to passes," as Philadelphia talk (pronounced twawk). The resonance of the Books of Moses, the cadences of the Psalms, the lucidity of the Gospel of John, the soaring rhapsodies of Paul on the love of God, the strange figures of the Book of the Revelation, all sank deeply into my heart and mind. Everything in life, I believed, had meaning as it related to what I knew of The Book.

There were many books in our home by and about people who lived by the Bible. It was in Amy Carmichael, a missionary to South India, that I found the kind of woman I wanted to be. She was at work for the Lord (an Anglican, she had founded a place for saving little girls from temple prostitution), and she took time in the midst of this to write of her experience as she walked by faith in a place where almost no one shared that faith.

A friend gave me *The Imitation of Christ* when I was in college, and I read it slowly, finishing it the following summer during evenings in a university stadium where I climbed up to watch the sunset.

One year when I was tutoring I came across, in the library of my pupils, a dull-looking novel called *Salted With Fire*. I had never heard of George MacDonald, but his writing gave me a whole new vista of the love of God. There was a shining quality to it, and a deep humanity. C. S. Lewis, I later learned, had found it, too, and did an anthology of MacDonald's work.

The biographies of missionaries—Hudson Taylor of China, James Fraser of Lisuland, David Brainerd of early New Jersey, Raymond Lull of North Africa—influenced the course of my life. Sometimes, if we can catch the sound of music that other people march to, we can fall into step.

It was when I lived in the jungle that books were hard to keep. Mold, mildew, crickets, and smoke did their worst, and I did not always have a way to transport more than one or two books at a time, or a place to keep them other than an Indian carrying net hung under the thatch. But they became even more precious, more indispensable in times when I had little contact with English-speaking people. I got around to reading some great books then—Tolstoy's *Anna Karenina*, Teilhard de Chardin's *The Divine Milieu*, Isak Dinesen's *Out of Africa*. Each spoke to me in some powerful, personal way.

Kafka said that books should serve as "the axe for the frozen sea within us." Tolstoy showed me my own vulnerability and need of redemption—as Flannery O'Connor does, too, in her "stories about original sin," as she describes them. De Chardin illuminated for me the immanence of God. Dinesen reveals majesty and dignity in human beings and animals as creatures of God, and the laughter at the heart of things. (In one book,

Seven Gothic Tales, she touches the courage of the Creator, the power of women, a herd of unicorns, the reason for seasons, the dogs of God, angels and chamber pots, coffee and the word of the Lord, and Mary Magdalene on Good Friday Eve. Imagine the humor and courage it takes to put all that in seven stories!)

A reader understands what he reads in terms of what he is. As a Christian reader I bring to bear on the book I am reading the light of my faith. "All things are yours, for ye are Christ's, and Christ is God's," said Paul. Browning's "Fra Lippo Lippi" expresses it this way:

> . . . This world's no blot for us, nor blank;
> It means intensely, and means good:
> To find its meaning is my meat and drink.

— 13 —

Flesh Becomes Word

Isak Dinesen in *Out of Africa* tells how she was sometimes asked to sit in on a Kyama, an assembly of the elders of the farm, authorized by the government to settle local differences among the squatters. After a certain shooting accident she had to write out a statement, dictated by a man named Jogona Kanyagga, regarding events leading up to the accident and proving his own right to claim the victim as his son. When the long tale was told (during which Jogona sometimes had to break off, hold his head in both hands, and gravely slap the crown of it "as if to shake out the facts") the baroness read it back to him. As she read out his own name, she writes, "he swiftly turned his face to me, and gave me a great fierce flaming glance, so exuberant with laughter that it changed the old man into a boy, into the very symbol of youth. Such a glance did Adam give the Lord when he formed him out of the dust and breathed into his nostrils the breath of life and man became a living soul. I had created him and shown him himself, Jogona Kanyagga of life everlasting. When I handed him the paper, he took it reverently and greedily, folded it up in a corner of his cloak and kept his hand upon it. He could not afford to lose it, for his soul was in it, and it was the proof of his existence . . . the flesh was made word."

Words are inadequate, we say. So they often are. But they are nonetheless precious. "A word fitly spoken is like apples of gold in pictures of silver." In a time of crisis we learn how intensely we need both flesh and word. We cannot do well without either one. The bodily presence of people we love is greatly comforting, and their silent companionship blesses us. "I know I can't say anything that will help, but I wanted to come," someone says, and the word they would like to speak is spoken by their coming. Those who can't come send, instead of their presence, word. A letter comes, often beginning, "I don't know what to say," but it is an expression, however inadequate, of the person himself and what he feels toward us.

Before Eve heard the voice of the serpent summoning her to the worst possibility of her being, before Adam heard the voice of God summoning him to his best, the Word was. The Word was at the beginning of things, the Word was with God, the Word was God. That Word became visible in the flesh when the man Christ came to earth. Man saw him, talked with him, learned from him, and when his flesh was glorified and he returned once more to his Father, men declared what they had seen. "That which was from the beginning, which we have heard, which we have seen with our eyes, which we have looked upon and touched with our hands concerning the word of life . . . we proclaim also to you." That eternal Word had become flesh and through those who knew Christ that flesh had become once more Word. Those who hear that Word today and believe it begin to live it and again it becomes flesh.

If I had a choice, I would not want to do without either the word or the flesh. I want letters from my friends, but I want to see their faces. I see them, but then I want them to say something. I have a guest book in which I always ask people to write their names, explaining that they need not write anything more unless they want to, but I open it after they are gone in hopes that they will have written some word as well. "Say it with flowers," says the advertisement, but when the flowers come how eagerly we look to see what the card says.

When I come to God I want words. Even though "there is not a word in my tongue but lo, O Lord, thou knowest it altogether," I want to say something to him. He knows what I look like, he knows my frame, remembers that I am dust. Does this flesh need words to speak to him? It does. There is, of course, a silence that waits on God. There is a lifting up of hands that takes the place of words. But there are times when we want desperately to speak. "Each in his own words" is all very well if you can find them, but often I find them only in the words of others.

I am troubled by the tendency today to assume that one's own words are "better" or more sincere than someone else's. The bizarre wording of wedding invitations I have received makes me want to go and hide rather than "share the joy." I did actually attend a wedding ceremony composed ("created" was what they called it) by the couple themselves, complete with prayers of their own making for the minister to read. This was somehow supposed to surpass the words of the Prayer Book. It didn't. Surely it is possible to repeat in all honesty expressions which others have found to be adequate which are at the same time both noble and beautiful? Doesn't it draw one out of himself, beyond his own horizons, to participate in an ancient ceremony? Does it really follow that the substitution of something "original" makes the thing richer?

Take the Psalms. They are human cries. Whoever wrote them knew the bottom of the barrel. He had felt his bones rot. He had sunk in slime, been ridden over, torn in two, betrayed, outraged, and bludgeoned. He knew the sweeping barrenness of loneliness, the forsakenness of grief, the bewilderment of unanswered prayer, and put them all into words that speak to my condition. So I read them back to God—with the expressions of faith and praise that punctuate the howls. "My heart is in anguish within me . . . horror overwhelms me . . . he will deliver my soul in safety from the battle that I wage" (Psalms 55:4, 5, 18); "My wounds grow foul and fester because of my foolishness . . . but for thee, O Lord, do I wait. It is thou, O Lord, who wilt answer my prayer" (Psalms 38:5, 15); "The earth reeled and rocked . . . but the Lord was my stay" (Psalms 18:7, 18).

How poor my own words would be compared to those of the Collect for Evening Prayer: "Lighten our darkness, we beseech thee, O Lord; and by thy great mercy defend us from all perils and dangers of this night; for the love of thy only Son Our Saviour Jesus Christ." I would be hard put to improve on Paul's prayer for the Roman Christians when I am praying for my friends (as an old lady in Canada used to pray for me, and included this prayer in nearly every letter she wrote me): "May the God of hope fill you with all joy and peace in believing, so that by the power of the Holy Spirit you may abound in hope."

Hymns are a powerful source of strength to me. Who of us can match words like William Williams' "Guide me, O thou great Jehovah, pilgrim through this barren land" or Henry Twell's "Thy touch hath still its ancient power; No word from thee can fruitless fall; Hear in this solemn evening hour, and in thy mercy heal us all"?

In the old words of George Herbert such as "Love bade me welcome, yet my soul drew back" or in the more modem poetry of Amy Carmichael: "And yet we come, Thy righteousness our cover, Thy precious blood our one, our only plea; And yet we come, O Savior, Master, Lover—To whom, Lord, could we come, save unto Thee?"—in such words my own flesh (empty, dumb, aching, needy as it may be) becomes, to God, word.

— 14 —

Spontaneity

A boy of two was standing in a bright square of sunlight in my kitchen one morning. He lifted his hands in the slanting ray that streamed through the open door. Then he lifted his face to me—a round, sweet face with a broad smile, lit with the sun and the light of discovery. "Look at these sunshine crumbs, Aunt Betty!" he said.

That was a spontaneous remark. Spontaneity may produce some delightful results, but for something to happen spontaneously it is necessary that certain conditions be present.

The little boy's observation does not arise, "out of the blue," but from a personality which, even at two years of age, has already been shaped by his parents, where he lives, what he hears, how he is trained and treated.

His mind is ready and eager to receive impressions and searches at once for words to capture those impressions. His vocabulary is limited, but he knows sunshine, and he knows crumbs—so in a flash he has given a name to the thing he sees.

His fingers reach out and touch nothing. Crumbs you can touch. Sunshine crumbs, he finds, you can't touch. He has absorbed all this in a second and has made it forever his own, making it at the same time his Aunt Betty's.

I was in a Laundromat one hot summer morning in Missouri. An old woman in a cotton dress, bobby socks, and thick-soled shoes was doing her wash and greeted me cheerfully. We talked about the weather, and I told her I was from Massachusetts. When her husband came in she told him the lady was from Massachusetts, and he said the weather back East had been bad, hadn't it, and that he had been back East once.

"During the War. We was in Atlantic City, New Jersey, and they made us march on that boardwalk that goes along there by the ocean, you know that boardwalk. Well, the guy in front of me—there was a little bitty patch o' ice on the boardwalk—and the guy in front of me when he come to that patch o' ice he fell right flat on his face. And we marched on down to the end of the boardwalk and turned around and marched back again and that guy fell flat on his face again when he come to that same little bitty patch o' ice."

That was the man's conversation, in its entirety. I thought about it for quite a while afterward. It always interests me to see just what it is that triggers people's remarks. Spontaneous action, the dictionary says, occurs, or is produced, within, of its own energy or force.

The old man's story, called to mind by the ideas of weather or of "back East" was spontaneous enough—not profound, of course, but the story and the images came out of the rich soil of his vivid experience.

Something had happened to him; his telling of it was straightforward. He wasn't concerned with the kind of impression he might be making on me. He was brief, and so clear that I'll never forget that scene during the war, the man himself, his wife, or even the Laundromat in that hot little town.

Spontaneous action may also mean "without premeditation," and this was true of what both the little boy and the old man said. Too often we are overly self-conscious; we play roles. Recently I saw a young man on television whose performance did not delight me. It depressed me.

He said, "As opposed to for example in other words in terms of borrowing from a loan company, you'd do better at a bank." He hadn't meditated much on that one. He was thinking about the setting, not about the subject.

The conditions which created his "spontaneity" were (1) the talk-show format, where you have to talk, and you have to put on a show; (2) a time allotment, which means the poor man had to keep on talking without pausing to think what he was saying; and (3) the man himself—trained to value such meaningless phrases as "for example," "as opposed to," "in other words," and "in terms of" because he thinks they sound learned.

The man was also quite conscious of his own image in the TV monitors and had little leisure for looking clearly at the matter at hand as my nephew had looked at the dust flecks.

If spontaneity implies the existence of an inner energy to begin with, one felt that his energy had petered out by the time the man delivered his remark.

I'm being hard on him, and he was, as I have said, young. Carlyle wrote of nineteen-to-twenty-five-year-old youths that they had reached "the maximum of detestability." We have been telling ourselves that youth is beautiful and spontaneity one of the most beautiful things about youth. I wonder if spontaneity is not sometimes a euphemism for laziness—an indulgence which Carlyle found in youth. Isn't it much easier not to prepare one's mind and heart, not to premeditate, simply to have things (O, vacuous word!) "unstructured"?

If you leave a thing altogether alone in hopes that it will happen all by itself, the chances are it never will. Who learns to play the piano, wins an election, or loses weight spontaneously?

I have just read Jean Nidetch's book on the Weight Watchers, and while it is obvious that her basic theme (that people get fat because they eat) is hardly a world-shaking discovery, her method is one that made her a millionaire: get people to work at their problems together. Reducing doesn't just happen. It isn't a thing the majority succeed in doing all by themselves.

She doesn't let them make up their own diet as they go along—that's what put the fat on them in the first place. She doesn't suggest that losing weight is best done when you feel like it. She doesn't even say that it works only if you are being "yourself."

In fact, I was reminded throughout the book of how many analogies there are between losing weight and practicing Christianity. There are rules to obey. You *will* to obey them. Some people insist that the devotional life is somehow purer or better if it is pursued only when we feel like it. Worship for some is thought to be an "experience" rather than an act. Losing weight is also an experience—there's no doubt about that—in fact, the expression "being born again" occurs in the testimonies of those who have done it. But losing weight most certainly has to begin with an act.

It is an act of the will. You decide to do *this* and not to do *that*. You must arrange, prepare, and carefully carry out your plan. The combustion of those daily calories will happen without fail, but only when the conditions are properly set up.

Love is another thing. "But I want it to be spontaneous," people say. They think that if nothing is happening it is good enough reason for a divorce. "If it isn't spontaneous, it isn't love," they tell us. Where did that idea get started? Do we understand what spontaneity requires?

The kind of love the Bible talks about is action, and it comes from a force and an energy within. That energy is the love of Christ. His love creates the condition of heart (it does not come from nowhere) which enables us to do things: to give a cup of cold water, to go a second mile, to "look for a way of being constructive," as Phillips' translation puts 1 Corinthians 13:4.

"It is, in fact, the one thing that still stands when everything else has fallen."

Christian love is a far cry from a misunderstood spontaneity which is merely unstructured. This love is a very firm and solid thing indeed, requiring will, obedience, action, and an abiding trust in the "Strong Son of God, Immortal Love."

— 15 —

Thinking

Question-and-answer is a vanishing art. We are so drowned and smothered and deafened by panels, dialogues, rap sessions, discussions, talk shows, and other such exercises in the pooling of ignorance that, far from developing the art of asking questions and giving answers, we have very nearly lost it altogether. The time allotted for a program must, it seems, be filled—it doesn't much matter with what.

When is the last time you heard a clear, short question asked and a straight answer given? My heart sinks when it is announced that, following the lecture, there will be time for discussion. People put up their hands, but it turns out that it is not information they are after at all. They want the floor. They go on and on.

I was one of the panel of experts (i.e., married women) discussing the subject of marriage in a college women's dormitory a few years ago. Afterward there were lots of questions. But it was hard to figure out just what the questions were. Here is one of them (*verbatim*—I did not make this up. It was taped and then transcribed):

> Um—like—um—I have a couple questions. Do you think—like—that—uh—do you think a woman could have a call just to be—like—a wife, but not—like—not just to be a wife—like, say, you know—if you're gonna be personal—like—my own engagement—like—I have a gift of—you know—a talent in music, you know—like—I mean, I know you're not saying—like—you know, especially in that case, I mean, you're saying more like—you have—like—I think our greatest thing in common probably is—um—is that—you know—is the dedication to serve God—you know—in the desire to, to follow—you know—to do his leading and—like—neither of us, you know, and especially in this kind of life you don't have a blueprint of what you—what he's gonna be doing necessarily, you know—and I'm just kinda concerned because like—you know—I've even thought about that cause I've kinda had a conflict—you know—growing up that way—you know—I'm talented musically—you know—so therefore I should probably look for somebody that's talented musically but he—he likes it—you know—I mean, he doesn't understand it totally but I'm sure we could live happily together with it, you know, but I don't expect him to have a—you know—yearning to go to all the Beethoven concerts or anything—you know—but I mean—I've heard of very happy marriages where—you know—there's quite different—you know—interests—you know—there.

(I apologize for not knowing the rules of punctuation for this kind of English.) Nobody on the panel knew what the girl was asking. She was confused—that came through loud and clear, but she might have seen through some of the fog simply by making the effort to clarify and shorten her question.

Sometimes I have been tempted to tell the audience that only questions of twenty-five words or less will be entertained. But I don't want to put people off any more than I can help.

William Strunk, Jr., in his wonderful little book, *The Elements of Style*, gives this advice:

> To air one's views at an improper time may be in bad taste. If you have received a letter inviting you to speak at the dedication of a new cat hospital, and you hate cats, your reply, declining the invitation, does not necessarily have to cover the full range of your emotions. You must make it clear that you will not attend, but you do not have to let fly at cats. . . . Bear in mind that your opinion of cats was not sought, only your services as a speaker. Try to keep things straight.

Americans dearly love to be polled for opinion. They feel that they ought to have opinions, to "hold views," on everything, and polls give them a chance to let fly. It is interesting to note how small a percentage of those polled admit to having "No opinion."

If the answer is Yes, say Yes. If it's No, say No. (The Bible will back me up here.) If it's I don't know, say that—if you possibly can. My daughter had a classmate in the seventh grade who, when asked a question by the teacher, never raised his chin off his hand, but looking into space said glumly, "I don't know." To a second question he replied, in the same laconic tone, "I don't know that either." I couldn't help wanting to know which boy that was. I liked him. It was discouraging for the teacher, I'm sure, that he didn't know, but it was not nearly so discouraging to hear him say so in three words as it would have been to hear three hundred words which came to the same thing. Every day in the mass media we have to listen to palaver, twaddle, and balderdash which, when interpreted, means "I don't know."

Some people are constitutionally incapable of admitting they don't know. "Well, let's just say I don't know the answer to that one," a woman once said to me.

Great people, however, can often disarm us completely with a candid acknowledgment such as Samuel Johnson's when asked by an indignant woman whatever made him define *pastern* as he did in his lexicon. "Ignorance, madam, pure ignorance!"

The Quechua Indians of Ecuador have a way of dropping the corners of their mouths, thrusting out their chins, and gazing off across the treetops, saying "Hmm hmm?" which is supposed to convey the impression that the matter is a mysterious one which they are in on but which would really be beyond you. At other times they come up with ineluctable answers like the one a missionary got when he wanted to know the name of a tree with yellow flowers on it. The Indian studied the tree for a little while, shading his eyes with his hand, and then said earnestly, "Well, I'll tell you, Señor Eduardo. That tree over there, the one you point to, the tree with the yellow flowers on it—that tree, Señor Eduardo, we call The Yellow Flower Tree."

The late W. H. Auden once appeared in a television interview and it was delicious to see his interviewers thrown completely off balance by the clarity and the brevity of his answers. They had their questions carefully worked out and the timing approximated, but long before the show was over they were casting about for new questions. When they asked if he thought of poetry as a means of self-expression, he said, "No, not at all. You write a poem because you have seen something which seems worth sharing with others. The ideal reaction from the reader is, 'I knew that all along, but I never realized it.'" He could, I am sure, have lectured for an hour on that one subject, but he didn't. He had a sense of occasion.

"You will be living in Oxford, England, Mr. Auden. Do you expect to be teaching there?"

"No."

"You won't be teaching. [Pause.] Well, Mr. Auden, as you move into the more—shall we say—mellow years, would you say that you have any unfulfilled ambitions?"

"No."

One of my unfulfilled ambitions was to hear a simple answer on a TV talk show. Thank you, Mr. Auden.

— 16 —

Observation and Silence

On a beautiful cool morning last July, Lars and I left behind all our usual work and chugged out of Gloucester harbor in Massachusetts on a fifty-foot fishing boat. There were about twenty of us aboard, all of us in high spirits until the captain announced that the marina we had just left as well as the restaurant behind it and the lobster packing plant next to it had been bought the previous day by the Reverend Sun Myung Moon. This lowered our spirits momentarily, but they soon shot up in anticipation of what we were about to see. It was not the cormorants that flocked on the tiny island at the mouth of the harbor, or the reef of Norman's Woe where the *Hesperus* was wrecked, or the lighthouse on Eastern Point.

We noted all of these things with interest (the oldest paint factory in the country did not rouse us much), but none of them were what we had paid our fifteen dollars apiece to see. Lars had called the week before to inquire about the advertisement. Did they guarantee anything? No, that was impossible, but in the twenty trips made so far that summer they had seen them every time. We decided it was well worth risking the price of tickets if there was even an outside chance of seeing them: whales. Not captive in Marineland, not doing tricks in the zoo, but real live full-sized unbelievable wild whales out in the open Atlantic Ocean, free-swimming, God-glorifying giants of the deep.

Our on-board whale authority turned out to be a man of about twenty wearing a T-shirt and cutoffs, with a baseball cap clamped over his long hair. He stood up in front of us with a chart and proceeded to show us pictures of "the whales we'll be seeing."

Well, I thought, *he sounds wonderfully confident. Will we be so fortunate as to see even one spout in the distance?* Sometime after half-past nine, he assured us, we might begin to spot them. We would understand the lookout's directions if we imagined the boat as the face of a clock, its bow representing twelve o'clock, its stern six. He then explained that the whales most likely to be in the area were the humpback and the finback, each having a characteristic "blow." Whales, being mammals, breathe air. They surface every few minutes, exhale a great column of vapor (the finback's is twenty feet tall, straight up into the air), inhale in a split second, and then dive.

They do their mating in the area of the Dominican Republic in the wintertime but eat little then. In the summertime they come north and do most of their eating off the coast of Massachusetts, occasionally going as far north as Newfoundland, depending on where the food animals are swarming. Instead of teeth these two species of whale have what is called baleen, a double series of triangular horny plates on each side of the palate (as many as six hundred all together) which fray out into a sort of hairy fringe to form a sieve which filters out of the ocean's soup all the nourishing tidbits such as plankton, krills, copepods, herring, sardines, and copelin.

The most remarkable of the tidbits is a creature called a diatom. These microscopic machines behave in some ways like animals (they swim and dig) and in other ways like plants.

Scientists cannot agree on how to classify them, but whales love them and they provide more food than any other living thing, nourishing not only whales but a variety of infinitely smaller creatures like krills (I confess I had never once wondered what krills ate). Diatoms come in several thousand species, in marvelous shapes (pinwheels, spirals, stars, triangles, chandeliers, discs, rods, ovals), and the largest of them measures a mere millimeter. A humpback whale consumes rather large helpings of diatoms, netting several hundred billion every few hours, taking in several tons of water with each gulp and straining these vast torrents through his baleen, as much as a million cubic meters of seawater a day.

Among our fellow passengers was a very large lady wearing a knit tank top and slacks which she filled to bursting. She had a shopping bag on what there was of a lap. We had not left our moorings before she had reached into the bag and switched on a radio, then began foraging for something to eat. Most of her crackers and bananas were gone, she had downed a Pepsi or two and inquired in vain if there was food to be bought, by the time the lookout cried, "Blow at eleven o'clock!" We rushed to the bow in time to see a distant geyser. The captain made for the spot, and soon we saw the huge glistening back and dorsal fin of a humpback roll to the surface and heard the surprisingly powerful *phooh* from the blowhole before it vanished.

Within a short time we had sighted other spouts, other fins, and then, to our great excitement, the monstrous tail or *fluke* splendidly flashed clear of the water so that we could see its markings and the clinging barnacles.

"There's your fluke, now," the captain's assistant remarked laconically.

Our knowledgeable young man had described something he called a "bubble net" which he hoped we might see. A whale goes down about thirty feet, blows a twelve-foot circle of bubbles so that the surface of the sea turns effervescent turquoise.

No one is quite sure why or how this works, but it seems to have the effect of confusing the small fish and other creatures so that they are "caught" in this net. About ten seconds elapse (the gulls have time to flock to the scene screaming, the eager watchers also scream and focus their eyes and cameras). Then, suddenly and awesomely, the whale's cavernous mouth explodes from below and swallows the "net" (and sometimes, the man said, an unwary seagull or two). We had seen perhaps three or four whales surface, blow, and disappear some dozens of times before the lookout shouted "*Bubble at seven o'clock!*" We raced to the stern, found a great green pool not many feet away, and held our breath as the enormous square warted snout of the humpback shot out of the water, the entire pool poured through the billowing mesh of baleen, and before we could blink in disbelief, the ocean was as faceless and empty as ever. I don't think anyone said a word unless it was "Wow." There would have been complete silence if it hadn't been for the sound of the radio in the shopping bag.

The lookout called our attention some minutes later to what seemed to be a patch of dim, pale-green light moving smoothly alongside the boat, perhaps four or five feet beneath the surface. It was the gray sidepatch of the finwhale. If he had not pointed it out, our uneducated eyes would never have noticed it, for there was not the smallest ripple, there was not the least sign to indicate that a fifty-foot giant weighing some sixty tons was accompanying us.

The fat lady, I think, missed it. She was eating another banana.

Not long after we had made this trip I received another of those letters from an aspiring writer. A young woman wrote, "I often yearn to be a writer but after reading books like yours, I feel that all the important things have already been said!"

They have indeed been said, and long before I said them. If a thing is true it is not new, but the truth needs to be said again and again, freshly for each generation. I have often been introduced to some seventeenth- or eighteenth-century writer by a nineteenth-century writer. If I quote what I learn from the ancients, a twentieth-century reader is sometimes helped when he would not by himself have found Crashaw's poem or St. Francis' prayer or St. Paul's Love chapter.

What of the twenty-first century? Which of the young people I know are now laying the groundwork for being the writers or artists or, as I like to think of any who show truth in any form, the prophets for my grandchildren's grandchildren?

I wrote to the young woman:

> Don't give up that yearning. During these busy years while you take care of small children and give yourself to being a godly wife and mother, lay the firm footing on which good writing must be built. Read *great* books if you have time to read anything at all. Get rid of the junk that comes in the mail, eschew all magazines and newspapers if your reading time is limited, and by "hearing" the really great authors, learn the sound and cadence of good English.

There are two other things required of "prophets." Observation ("What do you see?" Ezekiel and John were asked) and silence. ("The word of the Lord came to me.") Obviously we (I, at least, and most others, I suppose) are not anything like the biblical prophets. Ours is a different assignment. But we are charged with the responsibility of telling the truth, and I don't see how this can possibly be done without opening our eyes to see and our ears to hear. There must, there simply must, be time and space allowed for silence and for solitude if what we see and hear is to be "processed."

Antoine de Saint-Exupery, author of *Wind, Sand, and Stars*, said in a conversation with Anne Morrow Lindbergh, "The great of the earth are those who leave silence and solitude around themselves, their work and their life, and let it ripen of its own accord."

If any of the crowd we saw fishing from a breakwater as our boat entered Gloucester harbor again are among the "great of the earth," it will be against terrible odds. They, like the lady on board, were also listening to a shrieking radio.

In the cry of gulls, in the blow of a whale, in the very stillness of an early morning, it seems to me, we are more likely to hear the Lord's quiet word.

Speak, Lord, in the stillness,
While I wait on Thee.
Hushed my heart to listen
In expectancy.

— 17 —

Is There a Hero in the House?

The *New Yorker* carried a cartoon once which showed a pickup truck with the words *Haarlem Dike Emergency Repair Service* lettered on the door. In the back of the truck were six or eight small Dutch boys.

An exceptionally good joke, I thought. And it struck not only my funny bone but something deeper. All that business about the town of Haarlem being saved from destruction by the sacrifice of a boy in wooden shoes had thrilled me as a child. He had done the one thing possible when he put his finger in the leak. He suffered. I suffered with him as he stood through long hours, finger aching, then arm, back, and whole body racked and tortured. But he stood. He was "Hans, the Hero of Haarlem."

Does anyone do things like that anymore? Does anyone notice if they do? But this cartoon—can heroism be organized, commercialized, multiplied? If so, there isn't much thrill left in it. It's just a good joke.

Yet we still need heroes, and we need them desperately. I suppose it is partly because we are conscious of failure and ordinariness in ourselves, and we need to be cheered on by the sight of someone who is successful or extraordinary in one way or another. The classic hero of the past was a person of noble character, of fortitude in suffering, of unusual enterprise in danger. There came a time when the thing to do was to debunk all heroes, to smile tolerantly or even to sneer at what looked like greatness, and to attempt as loudly as possible to advertise the weakness of leaders. (Was it a relief to find that there was no need after all to praise anybody?) More recently the hero often hailed by the crowd is a nonhero, a man devoid of any quality of greatness. He is vapid and faceless and certainly not tragic, but only pathetic. Those who follow such a hero are pathetic, too, for he is unable to take them anywhere.

It is a bad thing to make something out of nothing. If there are no longer any real heroes, if the world has no chance for a glimpse of greatness, we shall in our bankruptcy have to make something out of nothing. Nonheroes, presumably, are better than no heroes at all. We have given up the outdated kind, the shining visions of knights in armor or towering kings who ruled in righteousness. We have new supermen: a Batman or a James Bond, whom we can get away with worshiping openly as long as we tell ourselves he's "high camp," or just a put-on. Quite without our realizing it, however, we have come to lump real heroes with Batman and 007. Heroism is nothing more than a put-on. To be *honest* nowadays is to recognize that one man is as bad and as laughable as the next, and the more thoroughly we can demonstrate his rottenness and his absurdity the more cheered we shall be as we contemplate our own.

We are all of us at times bad and laughable, but there are still also among us now and then truth, greatness, even holiness. The merest hint of true holiness we are quick to suspect as counterfeit, and we condemn what we like to call a "holier than thou" attitude. But years ago a teacher pointed out that the person I was condemning was in fact holier than I—and it certainly didn't take much.

George Eliot, in her incomparable novel *Middlemarch*, tells of a certain vicar who "had escaped being a Pharisee, but he had not escaped that low estimate of possibilities which we rather hastily arrive at as an inference from our own failure."

Because we ourselves bump along the low road, accommodating ourselves, compromising, making outrageously generous allowances for ourselves alone (such as saying, "That's the way I am, I have to do my thing," or calling old-fashioned, banal sins "frustrations" or "hang-ups"), we begin to find it less and less possible to believe that there really are some who travel a higher road and that they have reached it perhaps by genuine courage, sacrifice, or the kind of self-giving love that the Bible tells us about.

It is a bad thing to make something out of nothing, to make a hero out of a discouragingly common sort of person, or worse, out of one who has distinguished himself by degradation alone. Eliot's vicar did an equally bad thing. He made nothing out of something. Both errors come from the failure to value things as they truly are. We end up magnifying the trivial and minimizing the great.

I have written a book or two which have been taken by some of my readers as attempts to making nothing out of something, to debunk. A mere description of one event in one missionary's life (a conference on "the field") was read not as a description at all but as an attack on the whole scheme of modern missions, and even on the validity of Christ's great commission. "Are you determined," asked some wrathful readers, "to demolish the work of the Lord?" No, I had tried to recreate a scene. This is how it looked there, this is the way these particular missionaries spoke and acted. I had not tried to make it more or less than it was. "Are there no good missionaries?" questioned others. This question had me utterly baffled. A simple count of the characters in my book would have shown more goodies than baddies, or I don't know a goodie when I see one.

Later I wrote the true story of what happened in the life of a missionary who was nearly a hero by reputation during the latter part of his life, and whose death has, as often happens, made him a full hero to many. But some readers were convinced I had tried to make him a nothing; that I had searched meticulously for the negative aspects of his experience and personality in order to expose gleefully the feet of clay.

My model for this and an earlier biography had been the Bible. Men are shown there for what they are: far less than perfect, but far more than nothing. And a few readers, to my immense encouragement, wrote that they had been able to identify with Kenneth Strachan in my biography, principally because they had found him a man of "like passions" with themselves, a flawed human being, but one who had, in spite of his sins, sought the will of God. David, clearly shown to be both an adulterer and a murderer in the Bible, was yet a man whose heart was "perfect toward God."

An evangelical magazine carried a discussion not long ago on the missionary as hero. To say with a shrug, "Oh, this missionary hero bit . . ." implies that it's all nonsense. But to ask, "Are missionaries really heroes?" is beside the point. Some missionaries (and some knights, some sailors, some plumbers and housewives) are heroes, whether we like it or not. One of the writers in the magazine said, "The truth comes not through sentimental biographies peppered with anecdotes, but through facts." He was mixed up. The truth may indeed come through a sentimental biography peppered with anecdotes, for anecdotes, after all, may be facts, and very interesting ones, too. I for one would like it a lot better without the sentimentality. This cuts off some of the light. But an anecdote may well carry the truth of a man's life, as Jesus' parables showed heavenly truth, and may stun us into the awareness that we are looking at a great person: the man who did this, the woman who endured that. The abolition of heroes is easier said than done, for the world still contains them. Far be it from me to wish to debunk them. Just as far be it to wish to make a man look larger than life (which is what we mean when we speak artistically of "heroic" proportion). My job as a biographer was to try as hard as I could to show the man in life size, not smaller, not greater. This is impossible, for my own judgment is imperfect. Yet I try for it.

Let me remember his frailties, not to show him up as a mere put-on, but only so that I may not excuse myself from achieving what he achieved. If I regard him as invulnerable and blameless I shall take refuge in my own weakness and never aim at strength. Let me study his glory (whatever in him was really admirable) as a continual proof that men who were weak became strong, men who suffered passions and temptations that I suffer nevertheless rose above them. Even if they rose only for a moment, let me grasp the truth of that moment.

Recently I read in the paper that a woman was planning to sail the Atlantic alone. *Good idea*, I thought. If you like to sail, it would certainly be fun to sail across a whole ocean, and it might be interesting to sail it alone. I can easily sympathize with people's wanting to tackle a tough job, even if it's unnecessary, if it strikes them as a good adventure. (Men and women used to have real adventures in the ordinary and necessary course of their lives, but it doesn't seem to happen that way much anymore. We've inoculated and insulated and insured and protected ourselves against most kinds of adventure, so that we now have to go out looking for them.) The part in the news story that made me say, "Oh dear," was the announcement that the lone sailor was going to tape record her emotions throughout the voyage. *No*, I thought, *I don't want to hear about it*.

If the lady was going because she liked to sail, she might give us a good story when she got back, but if she was in search of an "experience" which would elicit certain emotions she was hoping to have, I doubt that the complete transcription would be something very many of us would like to hear.

Why is it, I wonder, that the question, "How do you feel about this?" has taken on such huge significance today? It is not a question concerning the thing done, or the purpose in doing it. People seem to have lost their objectives, to have forgotten what they are trying to do.

In the movie *Patton* the general encounters a soldier lying on the floor.

"What the —— are you doing?" he roars.

Leaping to his feet and saluting, the soldier stammers, "I'm just trying to get some sleep, sir."

"Well, get the —— back down on the floor, then," says Patton. "You're the only —— —— around here that knows what he's trying to do."

The question, "How do you feel?" strikes me as aimless. Suppose a clear answer can be given; then where are we? What do we know, in most cases, that is worth knowing?

The city of Boston had a Cleanup Day a few years ago, when thousands turned out on the Common with brooms, rakes, and plastic trash bags. A TV interviewer nabbed a teenage girl to ask the big question.

"I think it's beautiful," the girl answered. "I mean, you know it's like fun, a lot of people getting together and all."

"How does your mother feel about it?"

She shifted her gum to work the other side of her mouth. "My mother?"

"Yeah."

"Oh well," she said, "you know, she wished I'd, like, clean up my own room before I started on Boston Common. But, I mean, that's a typical mother reaction."

The girl laughed and went on sweeping and chewing.

Our sudden self-conscious effort in this technological age to treat people as people has made us act as though the be-all and end-all of life lies inside us, in our psyche, and as though the highest reason—often the only reason—for doing or not doing a thing is a feeling. I saw a poster put up by the youth group in a church which said, "If it feels good, do it."

For a few years I worked on some Indian languages in South America. I found in each of them a tremendous wealth of vigorous verbs and onomatopoeic words, but very few terms which describe emotion. How they felt about things was best discerned by what they did, not by what they said. I shared the emotions of the hunt not by the hunter's describing for me how he really felt during the chase, but by his telling me in detail where he was, where the animal was, what he saw, what he heard—the specific noises of the spear slicing through the air, the thunk when it sank into the flesh of the prey, the grunt or bleat or scream of agony as the animal was impaled, and the sound of the fall to the ground. The hunter was after food, not an emotional experience, but in this necessary work he found a huge pleasure which he managed also to give me just by the telling of the story. He experienced emotions which a man who hunted for the sake of the thrill would probably miss altogether.

It wasn't all thrills, of course. The Indian endured some terrific hardships, but he hadn't many words for those either. Weather was what I would call bad for hiking in the rain forest most of the time. But it was not talked about. The heavy burdens the Indians carried on their backs, the deep mud they plowed through, the steep hills climbed and ravines descended, the heat and gnats and thorns, were matters of course. They endured these without comment most of the time, doing what they had to do regardless of the difficulties, regardless of their feelings. They were far from unfeeling—I am convinced of this—though a superficial acquaintance with them might give the impression that they felt nothing. It wasn't that nothing mattered. They knew exactly what they were doing. Their aims were perfectly clear and those were what mattered. Feelings were simply not given much attention.

This is one of the things that made these people interesting. The trouble with hearing how everybody feels about everything is that after a while hardly any of it is interesting. No wonder talk shows are almost all the same. No wonder kids' faces are so expressionless. Everybody is looking inside. There aren't any horizons.

We hear a lot about the need for sharing. I am all for sharing what I have that others want, but too often the word means loading what we can't stand—our disappointments, hostilities, frustrations, burdens of all kinds—onto other people's shoulders. We ought to be willing, the Bible tells us, to bear one another's burdens, but each man is told also to bear his own. It is a big thing we ask when we lay them on somebody else, a thing not to be asked lightly.

A word no Indian language that I know has (and I wonder if it is nearly obsolete in our language) is *endurance*. Each time I read through the New Testament I am surprised at how often it occurs. "Sheer dogged endurance" is a phrase in Phillips' translation of 1 Thessalonians 1:3. Paul endured an astounding variety of trials. Jesus endured the cross—and the accounts of what happened that awful day are simple and stark: "There they crucified him."

But the idea of endurance in the Bible is associated with some wonderful words, too, I found. Words like *faith*, *patience*, *crown of life*, *hope*, *love*, *courage*. This is what it's about. The emphasis is on the ultimate object, not on how the sufferer actually felt in the middle of the night.

"Who for the joy that was set before him endured the Cross . . ."

Perhaps we can learn, as we grow, to pay less attention to ourselves and how a thing affects us.

"*He* hath borne our griefs."

That ought to be enough.

— 18 —

The Shock of Self-Recognition

Most of us are rather pleased when we catch sight of ourselves (provided the sight is sufficiently dim or distant) in the reflection of a store window. It is always amusing to watch people's expressions and postures change, perhaps ever so slightly, for the better as they look at their images. We all want the reflected image to match the image we hold in our minds (e.g., a rugged, casual slouch goes well with a Marlboro Country type; an erect distinguished carriage befits a man of command and responsibility). We glimpse ourselves in a moment of lapse and quickly try to correct the discrepancies.

A close-up is something else altogether. Sometimes it's more than we can stand. The shock of recognition makes us recoil. "Don't tell me that's my voice!" (on the tape recorder); "Do I really look that old?" (as this photograph cruelly shows). For me it is a horrifyingly painful experience to have to stand before a three-way mirror, in strong light, in a department store fitting room. ("These lights—these mirrors—they distort, surely!" I tell myself.) I have seen Latin American Indians whoop with laughter upon first seeing themselves on a movie screen, but I have never seen them indignant, as "civilized" people often seem to be. Perhaps it is that an Indian has not occupied himself very much with trying to be what he is not.

What is it that makes us preen, recoil, laugh? It must be the degree of incongruity between what we thought we were and what we actually saw.

People's standards, of course, differ. Usually, in things that do not matter, we set them impossibly high and thus guarantee for ourselves a life of discontent. In things that matter we set them too low and are easily pleased with ourselves. (My daughter came home from the seventh grade one day elated. "Missed the honor roll by two C's!" she cried, waving her report card happily.) Frequently we judge by standards that are irrelevant to the thing in question. You have to know what a thing is for, first of all, before you can judge it. Take a can opener—how can I know whether it's any good unless I know that it was made for opening cans?

Or a church. What is it for? Recently the one I belong to held a series of neighborhood coffee meetings for the purpose of finding out what the parishioners thought about what the church was doing, was not doing, and ought to be doing. The results were mailed to us last week. Eighty people participated and came up with 105 "concerns and recommendations." These revealed considerable confusion as to what the church is meant to be about. "Should have hockey and basketball teams." "There is too much reference to the Bible in sermons." "The ushers should stop hunching at the doors of the church and seek out unfamiliar faces." "The rear parking lot is messy." "A reexamination of spiritual goals should be carried out." I was glad there were a few like that last one. The range of our congregational sins was pretty well covered (we didn't get into the mire of our personal ones), and as I read them over I thought, "If we just managed to straighten out these one hundred and five things we'd have—what? Well, something, I suppose. But not a perfect church. Not by a long shot. If by our poor standards [some of them obviously applicable to things other than churches] we picked out over a hundred flaws, how many were visible to God, 'to whose all-searching sight the darkness shineth as the light'?"

There are times when it is with a kind of relief that we come upon the truth. A man passing a church one day paused to see if he could catch what it was the people were mumbling in unison. He moved inside and heard these words: "We have erred and strayed from thy ways like lost sheep. We have followed too much the devices and desires of our own hearts. We have offended against thy holy laws."

Hmm, thought the man, *they sound like my kind of people*.

"We have left undone those things which we ought to have done, and we have done those things which we ought not to have done."

This is the church for me, he decided. (I don't suppose a basketball team or a blacktopped parking lot would have persuaded him.)

"Put up a complaint box and you'll get complaints," my husband used to say. There is something to be said for airing one's grievances, and there is a great deal to be said for not airing them, but one thing at least seems good to me—that we be overwhelmed, now and then, with our sins and failures.

We need to sit down and take stock. We need mirrors and neighborhood coffees and complaint boxes, but our first reaction may be despair. Our second, "Just who does so-and-so think he is, criticizing the church when he never even comes to church?" And we find ourselves back where we started, setting our own standards, judging irrelevantly and falsely, excusing ourselves, condemning an institution for not being what it was never meant to be, and so on.

The church, thank God, has provided for us. There is Lent. It is a time to stop and remember. All year we have had the chance in the regular communion service to remember the death and passion of the Lord Jesus, and this once during the year we are asked, for a period of six weeks, to recall ourselves, to repent, to submit to special disciplines in order that we may understand the meaning of the Resurrection.

We are indeed "miserable offenders." We have done and left undone. We are foolish and weak and blind and self-willed and men of little faith. We run here, we run there, we form committees and attend meetings and attack the Church and its organization and its isolation and its useless machinery and its irrelevance and ineffectiveness. But all the time it stands there, holding the cross, telling us that there is forgiveness, that we have not been left to ourselves, that no matter how shocking the image that we finally see of ourselves in the light of God's truth, God himself has done something about it all.

"He was wounded for our transgressions. He was bruised for our iniquities." For the very things we've been discussing. For the things that make us moan and groan and ask, "What's the use?"

And so Lent, simply because it is another reminder of him who calls us to forgiveness and refreshment, makes me glad.

— 19 —

"M" Is for a Merry Heart

Special occasions like Mother's Day put different kinds of burdens on different people. Those whose work involves expressing themselves publicly usually feel that on such occasions they "ought to say something" appropriate to the day. At first I shied away from this, because I always shy away from things that might turn out to be soupy. But as I thought more about it I realized that it wasn't a question of "ought to" but a good excuse to write down just one or two things, at least, about a remarkable mother I know very well—my own. And if I write about her it won't be soupy.

She is nearly seventy-two years old now, and that fact, coupled with people's applying to her adjectives like "alert" and "spry" and "very much alive" remind me that she is in the category of "old." People certainly don't use those adjectives much for other age groups. But it is hard to think of Katharine Gillingham Howard as old.

She lives alone in a house in Florida between some orange groves and a golf course. She makes good use of the groves but she hardly has time even to look at the golf course, let alone play on it. Time does not hang heavy on her hands, and one of the things she does with it is to keep up a steady and cheerful correspondence with her six married children and her fifteen grandchildren. We write to her, make carbons of our letters, and she writes to all of us and sends the carbons around every week. She has taken a lot of teasing in her life with us, and we still tease her in letters and she teases back. She is one of those people who knows how to laugh, hard. When you stop to think of it, how many people in your acquaintance can laugh hilariously, until tears roll down their faces?

And one of the things we never let her alone about is the way she uses emotionally loaded words. Three of the six of us grew up during the Depression and were taught many small economies, including turning off lights and things. If Mother found a light left on where it wasn't needed, the light was *blazing*. A radio in an empty room was not just on, it was *blaring*. A child with no clothes on was not merely naked, he was *running around* naked. (Of course I'm not saying my mother is the only one who does this. People have asked me I don't know how many times, of the Indian tribe I knew in Ecuador, "Do you mean to say they just run around completely naked?" The idea of people doing quite ordinary things like sitting still or cooking with no clothes on seems to be a hard one to grasp.)

It was not possible, apparently, for Mother simply to take the children downtown. Children were dragged downtown and through the stores. If our friends came to visit us after school they *traipsed* through the kitchen, *traipsed* upstairs, *traipsed* through the bedrooms.

No matter how poor we were, my parents somehow contrived to have a guest room and it was frequently filled. Mother was a good hostess, and it seemed we were always meeting trains in Philadelphia or boats in New York that had missionaries on them, and we understood that it was a privilege to have guests in our home. Schoolboys who came home with my brothers on holidays from boarding school were in a separate category in my mother's mind, I think, though she was very sweet about having them. They were always *clattering* up and down stairs, *sloshing* around in the bathroom, and *bumping* down the halls with suitcases.

My father—very tall, very studious, and very fond of the outdoors—was not much good at all around the house, but occasionally he would try to spare Mother some work by fixing his own or, on very rare occasions, her breakfast. It never turned out especially well because she lay in bed, stark staring awake, and had to listen to him *rattling around* in the kitchen.

Mother's cooking was strictly sensible, plain and nourishing, and she was an expert at meat and potatoes. (She was raised, my father used to say, on roast beef, while he was brought up on fried smelts, Beauregard eggs, and jelly.) She had no time for fancy salads or dessert. Fresh or canned fruit and store-bought cookies were a fairly standard dessert because they didn't require *fiddling*.

When I came home from boarding school I felt that the menus at home were just too, too ordinary. "Well," said Mother, not much moved, "you just go ahead and do all the fiddling you want."

If she was talking about a shopping trip to Germantown, which she loved (she had grown up there and no one could ever convince her that there were stores elsewhere equal to Germantown's), she said she would "just run over there." If she was talking about one of my father's numerous speaking engagements, which were sometimes burdensome, he wouldn't run over, he would have to *trail way out* to Fox Chase or Doylestown.

A single woman named Daphne, who was always on the edge of financial ruin and therefore had to make do with a succession of battered old cars, never just drove to see us, she came *trundling* down the turnpike.

Well, it must have been quite a life for her. You wonder how anybody survives all the blazing lights, blaring radios, dragging of children, traipsing, clattering, sloshing and bumping, rattling around, fiddling, trailing, and trundling. Now that we have children of our own we know what she means, and increasingly appreciate the color and jollity of the life she made for us. We know, too, that there was a far deeper source of strength than her "merry heart" which, as the writer of the Proverbs said, "doeth good like a medicine." She often needed a great deal more than merriment—she needed a Rock that was higher than she. She found him, and with my father, she led us to him. We are grateful for that, and for what she put up with, and if you were to ask her now to tell about it, it would not sound chaotic or pitiable at all, I think. She would admit that she used all those vivid words, all right, but she would never have thought of them as loaded, and she would probably have to wipe her eyes for laughing at the pictures they recall.

— 20 —

Inklings of Ignorance

The sign that faces us as we arrive at the station says *Spor 1*. Let's see. I refrain from asking Lars this time—he must be weary of four weeks of my persistent questions about his language. In Norwegian *o*'s are usually pronounced "oo." Spoor. Related to the English word *spoor*? Of course: Track 1.

It's time to leave my husband's hometown of Kristiansand. The station is mobbed with kids with backpacks. The mobility of the student generation astonishes me. When I was their age I dreamed of a trip to Norway. Of all the countries of the world, it was Norway I most longed to see. Surely an impossibility. But here I am, and here they are, hundreds of them, chewing gum, none of them looking particularly wonderstruck. Their bright orange or red or blue packs crowd the platforms and waiting room. They wear colored striped jogging shoes, blue jeans, nylon hooded parkas.

A little boy with platinum-blond hair and apple cheeks eats popcorn while his mother buys the tickets. After a few fistfuls he carefully pours the rest on the floor. His mother turns, says something brief and mild, and walks out the door. He scoops a handful from the floor, stuffs it into his mouth, and follows her.

We board the train. Immaculately clean, windows sparkling, reclining seats with footrests and plenty of legroom.

Norway. The country that shaped my husband's childhood. He was like that little boy. His aunt, Tante Esther, showed me some snapshots of him at that age—the same round face, the same towhead. We have spent part of our time at Tante Esther's house, walking around the places of Lars' memories. We saw where the house and church once stood, saw the building where he, at the age of six or seven, plummeted over the bannister and down three floors on his head. We saw the park, the bakery, the bridge, the offices of *Faedrelandsvennen*, the newspaper he used to hawk on the streets. The rest of the time we were in a little cottage a few miles away on a beautiful inland waterway, Topdals Fjorden, where he fished many years ago with his uncle.

The train begins to move. We are in a tunnel in a minute or two and pass through many more as we travel westward toward Stavanger across a series of lovely valleys (Manda, Audnedal, Lyngdal—*dal*, I conclude must mean valley). Rivers, rocky mountains, broad green meadows, forests of spruce, aspen, birch, fir. Alongside the tracks I see bracken, buttercups, bluebells, lupine, and daisies as well as many bright-colored flowers I cannot name. Now and then we pass a small lake with grasses and water lilies growing around the edge. Moose country. I see a highway sign warning of a moose crossing.

It is not long before the passengers begin opening up their lunches. A man and woman across the aisle hand buttered rolls to their two grandchildren. They squeeze mayonnaise, shrimp, and caviar pastes onto the rolls from tubes, and gulp down large-sized soft drinks, warm from the bottle.

We watch the children, we smile, but they try not to look at us. You do not speak to strangers in Norway. Even Lars, open and friendly as he learned to be in Mississippi and Georgia, becomes Norwegian again, cautious, silent.

The four hours pass quickly. The roadbed is well maintained, as everything in Norway seems to be. The ride is very smooth. Lars dozes.

In the rocky pastures are sheep and cows. In the fields, curtains of hay drying on long poles supported at each end by X-poles. Stone walls separate the fields.

There are brooks tumbling through deep ravines and broad, smooth rivers meandering through the valleys. Two children skip in the shallows of a pebbly stream. Again I see Lars, and his cousin Bjorg, in the two children.

We arrive in Stavanger in time to see the *Queen Elizabeth II* just leaving her moorings and being towed slowly between the docks and oil tankers out to sea. We board a hydrofoil for the trip to Bergen. There is as much noise and vibration as there is in a bus, and the narrow seats, twelve abreast, allow as little legroom.

It is raining as we leave the docks. On all sides we see the monstrous dismembered anatomy of marine oil rigs. The man next to Lars points to the upturned feet of the one that capsized in the ocean some months ago, killing many men.

The vessel threads its way through miles and miles of nearly treeless, forbidding-looking islands, barely discernible through the cold fog that wraps us round. The islands are rocks, massive and smooth, rising abruptly out of the sea with a rim of black three or four feet high above the tide line, topped by a band of white—salt? guano, perhaps? A little greenery struggles for life in a few protected places in the rocks.

Is there ever any sun here? Who lives in these lonely places? There are very few houses. A man in yellow oilskins (only plastic,

I suppose) passes us in a little outboard. His dog balances himself on the bow, ears flattened in the wind, muzzle lifted.

It is a scene from countless paintings, evoking a strong sense of melancholy, of "Northernness." Latitude works, I am sure, secretly and powerfully within the personality of the artist. Also, it occurs to me, of my husband. Is this a clue to the deep reserves in him?

At every port there are storage tanks: Norol, Esso, Shell. Tankers pass us, all sizes, coming and going to the North Sea platforms. People in tiny rowboats ride their wakes.

The two children who were on the train with their grandparents are in front of us. They have started on a fresh round of rolls and pastes.

A beautiful blonde teenage girl with heavily made-up eyes sits on the arm of the seat across the aisles, bouncing in time to whatever it is she is listening to on earphones connected to a black box held by her boyfriend. She is wearing a splotchy faded denim jacket covered with American obscenities printed in colored ink, Wrangler jeans, cowboy boots, a T-shirt advertising Norwegian beer. She closes her eyes, rocks her head with the music, snaps her chewing gum. Then she speaks to her friend—in Norwegian.

Four old ladies sit in a row with shopping bags at their feet, clutching large pocketbooks, wearing the ubiquitous brimless hats of their age group. (Somebody told me Queen Mother Elizabeth made these popular. They were designed so that her subjects could see her face from all angles.)

What are the old ladies talking about? I can hear them, but I cannot understand a syllable. It brings back the feeling of desperation in missionary days when a "sound barrier" stood between me and the Indians, a great chasm I could not bridge. Lars understands them. His ability to speak with perfect ease a language I am perfectly ignorant of fills me with awe. He laughs at this, of course. "An easy language." Here is a whole world where he is at home and I am a stranger.

In the three-hour voyage there is no change of light. Clouds, gloom, yet we can tell that the sun has not gone down. At nine o'clock it is as light as it was at six.

We stay in the Bibelskolen Sommerhotel in Bergen. On each bed are a pillow, a bottom sheet, and an eiderdown encased as a pillow is encased, a wonderfully cozy arrangement we have found wherever we have slept in Norway. Breakfast is a feast—bread, cheese, goat cheese, salami, tomatoes, pickles, corn flakes, hot rolls, marmalade, jam, coffee and tea, all you can eat, included in the price of the room.

We wander around the open-air markets by the waterfront. They are filled with flowers, vegetables (one cauliflower costs five dollars), and oh, heavenly fish! Lars would rather smell fish than flowers. He cannot tear himself away from the beautiful clean rows of crab, shrimp, salmon, haddock, cod, and other varieties of seafood laid out on stainless steel. The men who sell them are no-nonsense types who wear rubber aprons and boots and wield wicked knives.

We board another train for Oslo. The station teems with thousands more backpackers. In fact, it is difficult to find anyone dressed as we are in street clothes or carrying suitcases. We both feel foreign now.

Again it is raining. We travel along a fjord where rock walls rise sheer above us. The spruces and firs drip with rain. The hay we see in an occasional small field is green and sodden on the racks.

Now a rushing river with weirs, now a green meadow where a lone fisherman casts his line at the edge. Bluebells, larkspur, cowslips, wild raspberry. I wish someone would open a window so we could smell them.

Dim, misty forests with open, moss-carpeted floors. No wonder Norsemen believed in trolls and hags! I expect to catch sight of them myself in this mysterious land.

Suddenly we see, through breaks in the clouds, patches of snow on the peaks above us. Then the view is blocked repeatedly by tunnels and snowsheds. The Bergensbanen (Bergen Line) has two hundred tunnels, three hundred bridges, and eighteen miles of snowsheds, the brochure tells us. The country between Mjølfjell and Myrdal is like the high bare country of the Andes or Scotland, a wild wasteland of snow, broken only where the wind has swept some of the black rocks clean. As we approach the lake at Taugevatn, where the altitude is over four thousand feet, a hiker moves slowly across the snow and two men in orange parkas huddle against the wind, mending a snowscreen. It is hard to realize it is July.

Then down toward Oslo. Miles of river, farms, valleys, fields of green things and bright yellow oilseed rape. The sun comes out intermittently, bringing campers out of their blue or orange tents along the riverbanks.

I will be glad when we board the plane tomorrow for London and Boston. I will soon be back at the desk in the comer of the bedroom, I hope a little humbler because, having seen a piece of Norway, I have received a little larger vision of God who made it and who loves and understands its people. New places of vision give me inklings of the magnitude of my ignorance—of the language, for instance, and of "things beyond our seeing, things beyond our hearing, things beyond our imagining, all prepared by God for those who love Him" (1 Corinthians 2:9 NEB).

I hope that I will have as well a little larger heart to love and respect the Norwegian I live with, who baffles and excites, nettles and amuses, annoys and cherishes me. A world I have barely glimpsed is home to him. What other worlds are in him that I have not begun to suspect? What revelations of glory do

I have to look forward to in the man whose meals I cook and whose laundry I do, when finally the image of God is fully restored?

"Who knows what a man is but the man's own spirit within him?" (1 Corinthians 2:11 NEB).

— 21 —

Early Lessons

When I was five years old I started to attend Miss Dietz's kindergarten, which was in a Methodist church just around the corner from our house in Philadelphia. On the first day of school my mother walked with me to the church. When she said good-bye she explained that when it was time to come home for lunch I was not to cross the street, but must wait on the sidewalk opposite our house and call her to come out and "watch me across."

Two things that I learned there (besides one song, "Here's the Baby's Ball") are clear in my memory now. I learned that life is unpredictable. The girl in front of me as we lined up for roll call suddenly threw up, covering Miss Dietz's desk and roll book. I learned also that people, myself included, are sinful.

I picked out a white china cat from the toy box and played with it every day, building a house for it with wooden blocks. One day another girl got the white cat first. I tried to snatch it away but she got up from her little wooden chair at the play table and raced around the room with the cat in her hand. I raced, shrieking, after her. My insistence that the cat was mine was of course not accepted by Miss Dietz, and I was, I think, punished—made to stand in the corner or something. Perhaps I was only reprimanded, but although I had been scolded and spanked many times at home, this was my first public humiliation and acknowledgment of guilt. No doubt that is why I remember it. I had expected to be known as, I had every intention of being, a good little girl, and I turned out to be a naughty one. Let no one laugh it off with "But you were only five!" or "A silly little thing like a china cat?" I knew very well that I was in the wrong.

The next year I began the first grade in Henry School. It was more than a mile from home and I covered this distance four times a day because I walked home for lunch. It was a solid, dismal brick building with a high black iron fence with spikes on it and a solid concrete school yard. I became acquainted with loneliness and fear. I started out with the unshakable conviction that everybody knew everybody else, everybody knew what they were supposed to do and where they were supposed to go. I felt that somehow I ought to know, too, but I did not know. I was lonely. I was also afraid. I was sure that I would not be capable of doing first-grade work and often lay awake at night crying about arithmetic.

Our teacher was always called "Mith Thcott" by the girl who sat next to me. Miss Scott was a lovely woman with a soft voice, soft white hair, blue eyes, and a gentle manner. As I remember, she wore only blue dresses. Sometimes when the sun shone through the high sashed windows Miss Scott would tilt and tum a crystal prism that hung on one of the shade pulls, thus casting a thousand rainbows around the dismal room. Occasionally she would give us permission to try to "catch" the rainbows and that forbidding schoolroom was transfigured into a place of color and laughter as we darted and lunged after the reflections.

Despite my fears I did learn where to go and what to do, and I managed to grasp first-grade arithmetic. But, I used to think, I could never do it without Miss Scott. Well, I was not required to do it without Miss Scott. Miss Scott was the teacher. Miss Scott was there precisely to teach me what I needed to know. It has taken me a good many years to realize that in the School of Faith, what I am required to do I am enabled to do. Provision has been made. I am not alone and there is nothing to fear, for "God can be trusted not to allow you to suffer any temptation beyond your powers of endurance. He will see to it that every temptation has a way out, so that it will never be impossible for you to bear it."

Valerie's first schoolhouse was a thatched roof on six poles. It had neither walls nor floors. It had no desks, no chairs, no blackboards. It was an Indian house and her schoolbooks came by mail from the States, delivered to our jungle clearing in a small plane two or three times a month.

I, of course, was her teacher and it was a neat trick to hold her attention when Indian kids hung over her shoulder (What are you doing?), picked up her crayons (What are these?), scribbled in the textbooks (Let me try that), smelled the paper (This is made of wood), and pestered her continually to come and swim or fish or hunt for honey or fly wood bees on a length of thread. It was what Malcolm Muggeridge would call a "scandalously desultory" method of education, and when we had struggled through three years of this I decided it was time for some peer pressure and a little more order. We returned to the United States and Valerie started the fourth grade in a small-town public school in New Hampshire.

I had arranged to have the school bus pick her up, but as she stood at the bottom of the driveway on the first day of school in her new school dress holding her new lunch box (and I stood at the top of the driveway with tears in my eyes), the bus passed her by. Poor little girl, I thought, remembering my own terrors. But she was made of different stuff. I drove her to school and she ran in with a light wave of her hand. "Bye, Mama! I can find my room all right."

It did not dawn on her for a couple of weeks that the teacher was talking to *her*, and therefore expected her to listen. Because for three years she had had my undivided attention, she assumed that the teacher was addressing only the others. When she got this straightened out she did her work acceptably.

When she was in the fifth grade a classmate inquired as to "what kind of sex" she had had. I gave her a hug (and silently thanked God) when she told me her reply: "I won't answer a question like that."

In the seventh grade she copied an answer from someone else's test paper. In tears she confessed this to me, we talked about the sin of cheating, and I went with her to make it right with her teacher. I was unprepared for the teacher's response of self-vindication. Incredulous that a student would acknowledge such an offense, the teacher assumed at the outset that I had come to accuse her of negligence. It took several minutes before she understood that Valerie had come to say she was sorry and was willing to pay whatever penalty the teacher might set.

In the tenth grade she took a certain amount of ribbing because she wore skirts instead of blue jeans to school. "You mean your mother didn't make you? You really *like* skirts? Because *what*? You like being a *girl*?" She was some kind of nut. When there was only one dissenting vote (Valerie's) when the civics class agreed that the legal voting age should be reduced to sixteen she was asked for an explanation. "Well, I just don't think we know enough to vote." Incredulous stares. Some kind of nut again.

Valerie's little boy will not be starting school for three more years. I look at the children waiting for the school buses today and wonder what will be dished out to them. Will it be alternate cognitive modes, multithematic creativity programming, subjective time-distortion learning, disinhibiting emotional patterning, kinesthetic self-actualization? Or will they find a few people left in the schools who haven't discarded common sense along with wisdom and morality? Will they learn how to read, how to write a clear English sentence, how to add and subtract? Is there still the possibility that somebody, somewhere will teach them to distinguish right from wrong?

But today's newspaper reminds us that this would be inimical to democratic principle. Morality, usually called "value judgments" nowadays, has no place, we are told, in public-school education, least of all in public-school sex education. Words such as *normal*, *ideal*, *masculinity*, and *femininity* must be expunged from teachers' vocabularies lest they inhibit the freedom of elementary-school children to choose a life-style, e.g., asexual, bisexual, homosexual, or even heterosexual. These choices are to be made, it is assumed, without any reference whatsoever to ethical responsibility, let alone to religious principles, let alone to any divine design.

Life can be unpredictable, lonely, and fearsome, as I learned in Miss Dietz's and Miss Scott's classrooms, because, as I also learned there, sin has entered into the world. Lest our hearts quail as we "tum our children loose," let us remind ourselves of the nature of the warfare in which we engage: "not against any physical enemy; it is against the unseen power that controls this dark world, and spiritual agents from the very headquarters of evil. Take your stand then with truth as your belt . . . faith as your shield . . . pray at all times." The weapons must be appropriate to the foe.

A prayer written by Amy Carmichael has been my prayer as long as I have been a mother, and I pray it now for my grandchildren:

> *Father, hear us, we are praying,*
> *Hear the words our hearts are saying,*
> *We are praying for our children.*

Keep them from the powers of evil
From the secret, hidden peril,
From the whirlpool that would suck them,
From the treacherous quicksand pluck them,
Holy Father, save our children.

From the worldling' s hollow gladness,
From the sting of faithless sadness,
Through life's troubled waters steer them,
Through life's bitter battle cheer them,
Father, Father, be Thou near them.

Read the language of our longing,
Read the wordless pleadings thronging,
Holy Father, for our children.

And wherever they may bide,
Lead them Home at eventide.

—22—

Christ's Parting Gift

Odd things turn up when you are moving. Last month when we packed up the things in the old house and came to this one, I found a slip of paper with my mother's handwriting on one side and Mrs. Kershaw's on the other. One day back in the fifties my parents were going for the day to Hartford, Connecticut (from New Jersey), to visit my aunt in the hospital. Mother wrote a note to leave for Mrs. Kershaw, the dear old lady who would be coming that day as usual to help with housework.

"Please get anything you want from the refrigerator to eat. If you have time perhaps you could roll out some brown sugar cookies. The house is clean so there is nothing to do in that line. . . . Thanks so much. Have a good day. Lovingly, K. H."

Mrs. Kershaw wrote on the other side, "The Day's Doings," and left it for my mother. Mother is pretty good at throwing things away (lots of people are poor at that), but she also knows what is worth saving. When I read over the scrap of paper I thought of our beloved Mrs. Kershaw. I have written about her before—a widow, stone-deaf, a godsend to our home, utterly without guile or self-pity, unfailingly cheerful, who quite as a matter of course gave herself to all of us all of the time. Her list seemed exactly the paradigm I had been looking for. I wanted to write about peace. Peace is one of those abstracts we refer to rather often, but seldom with much real comprehension. "The Day's Doings" helped me to get hold of what peace is.

The Day's Doings:

1. put my soiled clothes to soak
2. had my breakfast
3. washed clothes
4. prayed for all and Alice's recovery & home safe
5. washed up dishes
6. made a fruit cup good for all
7. wrote to [her son]
8. just opened my mail, came 10:30 A.M.
9. making cookies, rolling in paper
10. getting nuts ready for top of cookies
11. resting and prayer for all
12. fixing pie filling and crust
13. resting and lunch 2 P.M. I feel lost without you to eat with.
14. washing up
15. resting and reading
16. prayer
17. making Jell-O
18. washing up. No more eats.
19. baking cookies and pie
20. washing up kitchen floor last. 6 o'clock, not a soul here. I didn't even see a stray dog. Yet happy.

Here was a life without conflict. That is what peace is. It could be argued, of course, that she had it easy: a few little undemanding household tasks to perform, a nice house in which to perform them, people who cared about her, her basic needs met. Plenty of people in this world have that and more, but would give it all for five minutes of peace—the peace that characterized the life of our little old lady.

If she had wanted to look for causes for self-pity or depression, she wouldn't have had to go far. She was old and frail, slightly crippled with arthritis; she could not hear a single sound; she had a son who almost never called or visited her; she had lost her husband; she had very few of this world's goods. But she went through her daily routines with gladness, punctuating them with prayer. She had the peace of God, which is just as Jesus described it—"nothing like the peace of this world." It was his parting gift to the disciples and to any who will simply take it. "I give you my own peace" is what he said.

I was thinking of all this as I sat in the living room of the house we have just moved into. My books and notes were spread around me on the sofa, my clipboard was in my lap. In front of me was a vast expanse of Atlantic Ocean, framed to left and right by the fading colors of autumn woods and, at the foot of the slope between them, the raw and ragged edge of New England—a great jumble of giant rocks, bleached by the sun, clean—scoured by wind and tide. The sea itself, miles and miles of it, danced, glittered, and flashed. ("*Coruscated* is the word," my brother Tom Howard said on the phone when I tried to describe to him what I could see. He's been my thesaurus since he was about five.)

There was nearly perfect silence all day long. I could hear no traffic on the road. Occasionally I heard a plane, circling northeast to land at Boston's Logan Airport, or the soft thub-thub of a lobster boat's idling motor. I heard the lonely cry of seagulls and the thunder and sigh as waves broke and retreated, but it was a day full of *peace*. I reveled in it. I thanked God in every way I could think of.

But someone I love is in the hospital today, waiting for a diagnosis which, judging by the symptoms we know of so far, could be a grave illness. The kind of peace afforded by the quiet house set in such matchless beauty is not really enough. It is not enough for my heart.

In the same talk in which Jesus spoke of his peace, just before he left his disciples to return to the Father, he said, "You *must not* be distressed and you *must not* be daunted." How, Lord, can I possibly obey a command like that when trouble—serious trouble—stares me in the face? What does peace mean now? Is it merely a feeling of calm? Does it mean to be soothed or comfortable? Is it a vague sense of well-being?

I don't know anywhere to look for answers but in the same old Book. The Old Testament sense of the word *peace* is, among other things, perpetual prosperity, security of tenure, health, and freedom from annoyance. The list almost seemed a mockery. It would certainly be a mockery if we could see no further than natural things. The man who sees only those has a "carnal" attitude, Paul says, "and that means, bluntly, death." A spiritual attitude, on the other hand, means life and inward *peace*. The New Testament explains much more about this inward kind. It comes from God. It is a gift, the fruit of faith. It passes understanding. It is Christ himself. *"He is our peace."*

The peace of God means the absence of conflict with the will of God. It means harmony within, concord with his purpose for our lives.

Mrs. Kershaw was not merely adjusted to herself or her circumstances. She was, in the deepest place of her being, reconciled to God. She never took a sedative or a tonic in her life. Like the weaned child spoken of by the psalmist, no longer frantic for satisfaction, she was at rest. If you had asked her her secret, she would no doubt have given a little shrug and a little chuckle. The sweet old wrinkled face would have looked up quizzically. She would not have known what to say. She simply did what the Christians of Philippi were told to do: "Don't worry over anything whatever; tell God every detail of your needs in earnest and thankful prayer, and the peace of God, which transcends human understanding, will keep constant guard over your hearts and minds as they rest in Christ Jesus."

To *make peace* with a country or a person or God requires a transaction. To *have peace*, as people sometimes say, unless it is merely the sense of well-being that commonly goes with getting what you want, must mean that a transaction has taken place. One's will, along with everything else, has been offered up. Peace is the divine answer to our *Yes*, *Lord*.

Colossians 3:15 suggests that the peace of Christ is the "arbiter" of our hearts, ruling out all faithless response to trouble, all distress, anxiety, fretfulness, frustration, and resentment. It establishes order. Those who accept the grace of this gift know tranquility which can withstand all assaults, a stillness unbroken by the world's noise, and a repose in the midst of intense activity—repose which a nerve-racked world cannot possibly give. For only Christ himself, who slept in the boat in the storm and then spoke calm to the wind and waves, can stand beside us when we are in a panic and say to us Peace. It will not be explainable. It transcends human understanding. And there is nothing else like it in the whole wide world.

— 23 —

Fear, Suffering, Love

I happened to arrive home alone from the airport one night in the middle of what newscasters like to call an "outage." I much prefer to call it a power failure. I could have unpacked my suitcase and found something to eat by candlelight—I lived for years with no other kind—but there was a show going on which I did not want to miss. I sat by the window and watched a storm over the ocean—driving rain and nearly continuous lightning, flashing in a hundred places along miles of horizon. Sometimes great billows of stormcloud were thrown into relief by a bright sheet of light from behind. Sometimes jagged bolts of lightning cracked the heavens, stabbing the skyline of Scituate and Cohasset to the southwest (our house faces south from Cape Ann over Massachusetts Bay). The rain swept the deck and blasted the windowpane while thunder, one of the many voices of God, rolled and crashed.

> Where is the place of understanding? God understands the way to it, and he knows its place. For he looks to the ends of the earth. . . . When he made a decree for the rain and a way for

> the lightning of the thunder, then he saw it and declared it; he established it and searched it out. And he said to man, "Behold, the fear of the Lord, that is wisdom; and to depart from evil is understanding."
>
> Job 28:20–28

It is well that men should fear God when they have not yet learned to love him. It is the beginning. People who have loved him, even for a lifetime, do not lose but rather gain reverence and awe, even godly dread.

Lightning is several times associated with the Lord's appearances in Scripture. The face of the man clothed in linen who came to Daniel during his three weeks' mourning and fasting was "like the appearance of lightning, his eyes like flaming torches." The same is said of the angel that rolled back the stone from Jesus' grave. John had a vision of a throne in heaven from which issued flashes of lightning and voices and peals of thunder. When the angel of the Seventh Seal took a golden censer and threw it on the earth, "there were peals of thunder, loud noises, flashing of lightning, and an earthquake."

When Mt. St. Helens exploded, it poured volcanic ash on the Northwest which floated as far as our coast. I woke one morning to find the sea shrouded in a strange pinkish brown fog.

There have been earthquakes in California and Nevada.

People call such things acts of God. They are awesome and often terrifying.

What of the acts of men? A seminary student who was in the navy for ten years told me of weapons now perfected by the Russians which would enable them to win a war without killing millions of people, but simply by knocking out our arsenals and disabling our equipment. I saw a documentary film which graphically contrasted U.S. military strength to Russia's. Our position appeared extremely precarious. A "missile eater" impressed me most—a defense weapon Russia now has which seems to annihilate missiles, snatching them out of the air before they can reach their targets.

I am not afraid for myself. But I confess I am tempted to be afraid for my grandchildren. They are with me now, a boy of three and a girl whose first birthday will be this week. What will they suffer?

The signs God gives us of his power and glory (thunder and lightning, for example), to say nothing of the unimaginable forces which he puts into men's hands and allows them to harness for their own often evil purposes, are in themselves fearsome.

As I watched God's storm that night I thought of his wonderful name, Father of Lights. Then as I saw the distant marine beacons sending their beams across the waves, they reminded me as they do every night of the Father's mercy. We live in a world created by his almighty power but corrupted by man's pride and selfishness. We need a place of safety—as Walter and Elisabeth need a place of safety as they grow up. There is one, but only one. It is the Father's arms. He will not—indeed, if he is to redeem and make us holy, he cannot—protect us from all suffering.

George MacDonald, in his novel *What's Mine's Mine*, wrote:

> There are tenderhearted people who virtually object to the whole scheme of creation. They would neither have force used nor pain suffered; they talk as if kindness could do everything, even where it is not felt. Millions of human beings but for suffering would never develop an atom of affection. The man who would spare *due* suffering is not wise. Because a thing is unpleasant, it is folly to conclude it ought not to be. There are powers to be born, creations to be perfected, sinners to be redeemed, through the ministry of pain, to be born, perfected, redeemed, in no other way.

I am thankful that there are some earthly fathers who understand this. One of them wrote to me of a visit to the doctor with his three-year-old son who was limping as a result of a fall or a collision with a child in the church nursery.

"Walt was in the backseat as the two of us rode down to the doctor's. There, I told him to wait a minute while I checked to make sure the doctor was in his office. The receptionist told me I could catch him over at the hospital in the emergency room. I came out to the car and drove to the hospital.

"Walt III: 'Where we goin', Daddy?'

"'We're going to see if the doctor will check your foot out at the hospital. Won't that be neat?'

"(A pause.) 'Uh . . . Daddy, I think it'll be okay if we go on home. Yeah . . . I think it'd be better after while. Whyn't we just go home, 'kay?'

"'Son, we're going to go see if we can get the doctor to check and make sure everything is okay.'

"(A tiny hint of a whine.) 'Daddy, I'm sure it's gon' be better now, okay?'

"At the hospital: 'Walter, let's get out and go into the hospital. Everything is going to be all right. Just hold my hand.'

"In the emergency room he wanted to sit in my lap. The clerk asked the names and how we were going to pay, etc. Then the wait. We move to a row of chairs against the wall, and Walt III chooses to sit in my lap this time with more enthusiasm. His eyes are big and wide. He's very solemn, head moving around, taking it all in.

"'Daddy, we've been here before.'

"'Yes, Walt, we were here. Remember the time your leg was broken and Daddy put you in that green blanket and brought you here? The doctor looked at your leg and then they took you to take some pictures of your leg?'

"'Hunh.' (That means yes.) 'I 'member dat.'

"'Shall we pray together?' His head bows quickly.

"'Kay.'

"A prayer in which I asked for courage for both of us. And thanking the Lord that we could trust him. Walt III much more relieved, even calmed completely.

"A nurse calls his name, and we go into a room to be seen by the doctor. It was hard to keep from carrying him, but I wanted the doctor to see Walt's limp, and too, I kept saying to myself, 'Let's not smother him. Let's help him grow up and learn to lean on the Lord himself.'

"In the room we both sit on the table. I take off his shoe and sock (I was fearful that the original break was damaged again) and we hear a lady crying in the next room. Walt's eyes get wide and he says,

"'Daddy, what's the matter with that lady?'

"'She is hurting and she is scared. Are you afraid, son?'

"'No, Lord Jesus take care of me.'

"'Well, let's pray for her, okay?'

"'Kay.'

"A prayer. And sure enough, the lady seems to calm down. And the doctor's there now, asking Walt where it hurts. Then, off to x-ray. A nurse comes to talk to Walt.

"'Now listen—if we hurt you then you can cry. But if we don't hurt you, you are not to cry, okay?'

"'Kay.' She picks him up (he holds tightly to her, eyes very wide) and just before she takes him off he says to me, 'Daddy, we've been here before. Where you gon' be? In this room waiting for me?' (The x-ray process had terrified him when the nurse took him from us a year ago.)

"'Yes, son, I'll be right here, waiting for you.' Fifteen minutes later the nurse brought him back to me, raving about what a neat kid he was. Apparently he had kept talking to them the entire time.

"No bones broken. We go back to the doctor. I tell Walt to be sure and thank the doctor as we leave. Walt goes about twenty feet out of his way from the exit to say, 'Thank you, doctor. We gon' to family night supper at the church.'

"Next night he happily sang to himself in the dark for about thirty minutes. I went to the bedroom to hug him and tell him, 'Walt, I'm proud of you for three reasons. One, you were very sweet in the tub when Mom washed your hair. Two, you make me happy singing so nicely to yourself in the dark. Three. . . .'

"'But Daddy—you making too much racket!' Then he grabs me and hugs me, giggling.

"Thank you, Lord, for that boy!"

And thank you, Lord, for that father, strong in his faith in you, strong enough in his love for the little child to lead him also to trust you.

I am sobered by the response of a tiny boy. With reason enough to fear, he resolved not to. How often my own faith deteriorates into a mere condition, shaped by circumstances, rather than a calm resolve, founded on one whose word I have come to trust. Perfect love casts out fear.

And what of the weeping woman in the next room? Was she calmed? Would she have believed, if told, that the God of Peace had laid his hands on her—in answer to the prayers of a little boy with a hurt foot? The God who rides stormclouds is also the God of Peace. The one who makes darkness his covering is also the Father of Lights.

— 24 —

One of Those Nineteenth-Century Missionaries

"All generalizations are false, including this one," yet we keep making them. We create images—graven ones that can't be changed; we dismiss or accept people, products, programs, and propaganda according to the labels they come under; we know a little about something, and we treat it as though we know everything.

I couldn't count the times I've heard nineteenth-century missions and missionaries cited as examples of stupidity and failure. I heard a whole lecture predicated on this assumption. They were bigoted and imperialistic and naive and arrogant and hypocritical. Some of them probably were some of those things. Some twentieth-century missionaries might make the ones of the last century look like paragons by comparison. Missionaries are (and need we go over this again?) human like everybody else, but the world has seen some great ones, some men and women who saw something to which they witnessed with truthfulness and often with real sacrifice.

In a box of old family papers, I found a little frayed booklet put out in 1906 by the Yale Foreign Missionary Society entitled *A Modern Knight*, by Joseph Hopkins Twichell. It broke up some of my categories. It was the story of John Coleridge Patteson, Missionary Bishop of Melanesia. He was English ("of course," I said to myself—I think of nineteenth-century missionaries as English—my generalization).

He came from a refined English home. He was the nephew of the famous poet Coleridge and the son of an eminent jurist. He had his place "by birth," the booklet says, "in the upper circles of English society." Exactly. No categories shaken by those facts. He grew up in a "praying household, notably pervaded with the spirit of humble piety and with all sweet gospel savors. There is no mistaking the evangelical tone and quality of the religion there prevailing." He went to Eton, was confirmed in the Church of England, and graduated from Oxford, a "rarely accomplished scholar." He was elected fellow of one of the colleges of his university.

But instead of becoming a jurist like his father, John went as a missionary to the Melanesian Islands to work with people who were nearly all savages and naked and cannibalistic—a people marked by "features of repulsiveness and horrible ferocity," according to the chronicler. But it is interesting to note that Patteson himself spoke of them as *men*. To him they were "naturally gentlemanly and well-bred and courteous. I never saw a 'gent' [by which term I think Patteson meant one who vulgarly tries to imitate a gentleman] in Melanesia, though not a few savages. I vastly prefer the savages."

He saw that they spoke a language, not the "uncouth jargon of barbarians" as many assumed. ("They don't speak a language, do they?" people have asked me of Ecuadorian Indians. "They only make sounds.") Patteson considered some of the Melanesian languages better than English for translating the biblical Hebrew and Greek.

"He gave them his company," writes Twichell. "For years together he scarcely saw any human being save his handful of assistants and his dark-skinned Melanesians. He never married. He adopted that wild race as his family." It is Twichell who thinks of them as a wild race. Patteson "had none of the conventional talk about degraded heathen. They were brethren."

He was ecumenical in spirit, at one time having to assume charge of a mission of another denomination where he scrupulously conformed to the practices of that mission, though he admitted that he greatly missed the Prayer Book.

The nurture of the indigenous church has been thought to be a recent emphasis in missionary work. Patteson made this his primary object. He visited the islands for four to six months of each year, and spent the rest of the time instructing people of both sexes at a central location. He insisted that they return to their homes at the end of the instruction period as a test of their own progress.

Patteson himself was up against gross misconceptions of the nature of his work, but he wrote truthfully about it. "In these introductory visits scarcely anything is done or said that resembles mission work in stories. The crowd is great, the noise greater. The heat, the dirt, the inquisitiveness, the begging, make something unlike the interesting pictures in a missionary magazine of an amiable individual very correctly got up in a white tie and black tailed coat, and a group of very attentive, decently clothed, nicely washed natives."

Patteson could not abide sentimentality, that lifeless, heartless, and ultimately cruel idol of many Christians. "One who takes a sentimental view of coral islands and coconuts is of course worse than useless," he wrote. "A man possessed with the idea that he is making a sacrifice will never do. A man who thinks any kind of work beneath him will simply be in the way." He was to be found milking cows and cutting out girls' dresses and doing things the people in England thought shocking.

"Integration" was not a word in his vocabulary as we use it today, and he deplored "that pride of race which prompts a white man to regard colored people as inferior to himself. They (the natives) have a strong sense of, and acquiescence in, their inferiority ('Does an ant know how to speak to a cow?' one of them once said) but if we treat them as inferiors they will always remain in that position."

Progress reports? "My objection to mission *reports* has always been that the readers want to hear of progress, and the writers are thus tempted to write of it; and may they not, without knowing it, be, at times, hasty that they may seem to be progressing? People expect too much. Because missionary work looks like failure, it does not follow that it is. Our Savior's work looked like a failure. He made no mistakes either in what He taught or in the way of teaching it, and He succeeded, though not to the eyes of men."

Patteson saw his own work as seed sowing. He was prepared to wait long and patiently and not to dig up in doubt what he had planted in faith. He gave to the handful of Melanesians whom he was training a care of instruction and discipline that was "deliberate and painstaking beyond measure."

We have heard missionaries of the last century accused of transferring European civilization to the native culture as though it were synonymous with Christianity. Patteson said, "I have long felt that there is almost harm done in trying to make these islanders like English people. They are to be Melanesian, not English, Christians. . . . Unless we can denationalize ourselves, and eliminate all that belongs to us as English and not as Christians, we cannot be to them what a well instructed countryman of theirs may be. . . . Christianity is the religion of humanity at large. It has room for all. It takes in all shades and diversities of character, race, etc."

When he was little over forty, Patteson visited an island he had never been to. He was received from his ship in a native canoe and taken to shore. The crew waited hours for his return, and at last saw two canoes leaving the beach, one towing the other which appeared to be empty. Soon the empty canoe was cast adrift while the other was paddled rapidly back to shore. Cautiously the boat's crew made toward the drifting canoe. As they drew alongside they saw the body of John Coleridge Patteson, wrapped in a mat, a palm frond laid on his chest. It was the year 1871.

The church, for the most part, has forgotten this name in the long list of its martyrs. It forgets most of what has been done and suffered, and thinks it is doing and suffering now as never before. We boast of our progress (from missions to "mission," for example) and criticize those bunglers of one hundred years ago. But criticism is an easy-chair exercise, especially when the critic does not trouble himself to look at the data but relies chiefly on what he himself feels or on "what everybody knows"—on generalizations.

Thank heaven the work of Patteson and all other missionaries, as well as the work you and I have to do today, is subject to the judgment of "a judge who is God of all," who never mistakes the counterfeit for the real, never needs to revise his categories, never lumps men together.

—25—

Women in World Missions

A Talk Given to Students at Urbana, Illinois, 1973

Years ago I had the great good fortune to meet an unforgettable character whose biography is entitled *The Small Woman*, and whose life story was told, after a fashion, in a movie called *The Inn of the Sixth Happiness*. She was Gladys Aylward. To hear this little creature of four feet eleven inches, dressed as a Chinese, tell her own story in a stentorian voice was a stunning experience. I remember how she took the microphone and with no preliminary nonsense whatever thundered forth, "I should like to read just one verse. 'And Jehovah God spoke to Abram and he said, "Get out!"'" She told us the story of Abraham's faith and his move into an unknown land. Then she said, "And one day, in a little flat in London, Jehovah God spoke to a Cockney parlor maid and he said, 'Get out!' 'Where do you want me to go, Lord?' I said, and he said, 'To China.'" So Gladys Aylward went to China. And what a story that was—a train across Europe and Russia, a frying pan strapped to the outside of her suitcase, an angel's guidance in the dead of night onto a forbidden ship, a breathtaking saga of one woman's obedience to the call of God.

Some twenty-six centuries earlier, the word of the Lord came to a much more likely prospect than a parlor maid—he was the descendant of priests—and in a much more likely place than the city of London, Anathoth in the land of Benjamin. Isn't it easier to believe that the word of the Lord might come to somebody in Anathoth than in London? Or in Urbana? The man was Jeremiah, appointed a prophet of the nations, but he was reluctant to accept the appointment. "Ah, Lord God," he groaned. "Behold, I do not know how to speak for I am only a youth." But the Lord said to him, "Do not say 'I am only a youth,' for to all to whom I send you you shall go, and whatever I command you you shall speak. Be not afraid of them, for I am with you."

God's call frequently brings surprise and dismay, and a protest that one is not qualified. Jeremiah hoped he might get out of it by reminding Almighty God (in case Almighty God had not noticed) that he was too young. Gladys Aylward did not strike me as timid, but she might have called God's attention to her limitations: she too was young; she was poor; she had no education; she was no good at anything but dusting; and she was a *woman*. In the case of both prophet and parlor maid, however, the issue at stake was identical. The issue was obedience. Questions of intellect and experience, of age and sex, were quite beside the point. God said *do this* and they did it.

What is the place of women in world missions? Jesus said, "You (and the word means all of you, male and female) are my witnesses. *You* are the salt of the earth. *You* are the light of the world." And there have been countless thousands who, without reference to where they came from or what they knew or who they were, have believed that Jesus meant what he said and have set themselves to follow.

Today strident female voices are raised to remind us, shrilly and *ad nauseam*, that women are equal with men. But such a question has never arisen in connection with the history of Christian missions. In fact, for many years, far from being excluded, women constituted the majority among foreign missionaries.

Missionary, of course, is a term which does not occur in the Bible. I like the word *witness*, and it is a good, biblical word meaning someone who has seen something. The virgin Mary saw an angel and heard his word and committed herself irretrievably when she said, "Behold the handmaid of the Lord." This decision meant sacrifice—the giving up of her reputation and, for all she knew then, of her marriage and her own cherished plans. "Be it unto me according to thy word." She knew the word was from God, and she put her life on the line because of it. The thing God was asking her to do, let us not forget, was a thing that only a woman could do.

The early history of the Church mentions other women who witnessed—by ministering to Christ during his earthly work, cooking for him, probably, making a bed, providing clothes and washing them—women who were willing and glad to do whatever he needed to have done. (And some of you who despise that sort of work—would you do it if it was for him? "Inasmuch as ye have done it unto one of the least of these my brethren," Jesus said, "ye have done it unto me.") There was Priscilla, coadjutor of the Apostle Paul. There was a businesswoman named Lydia who opened her heart to what was said and then opened her home to those who said it. There must have been thousands of women like these who did what lay in their power to do because with all their hearts they wanted to do it. They had seen something; they had heard a word; they knew their responsibility.

In the conversion of the Teutonic peoples, women played an important role. Clovis, King of the Franks in the fifth century, made the mistake of marrying a Christian princess, Clotilda from Burgundy, and through her was eventually baptized. According to the Venerable Bede's account, King Ethelbert of Kent made the same mistake in the next century, and his queen, Bertha, persuaded him to allow a monk named Augustine to settle in Canterbury. Within a year ten thousand Saxons were converted.

One of the earliest of those who were actually called missionaries was Gertrude Ras Egede, a Danish woman. Although violently opposed to her husband's going to Greenland to try to find the remnants of the Church which had been lost for several centuries, she soon saw that her opposition to him was in reality opposition to God. She repented and went with her husband to what turned out to be a far cry from the "Green Land" they had expected. It was a frigid godforsaken wasteland, where Gertrude Ras Egede died after fifteen years of hard work—generally called "labor" if a missionary does it. (We all know that missionaries don't go, they "go forth," they don't walk, they "tread the burning sands," they don't die, they "lay down their lives." But the work gets done even if it is sentimentalized!)

Women in the United States began to swing into action for the cause of world missions in the beginning of the nineteenth century. There was a Boston Female Society for Missionary Purposes founded in 1800, and a Miss Mary Well founded what was called the Cent Society in 1802 "for females who are disposed to contribute their mite towards so noble a design as diffusion of the gospel light among the shades of darkness and superstition." There was a Fuel Society which paid for coal for young seminarians, a Boston Fragment Society which provided clothes for indigent mothers and their babies. Massachusetts and Connecticut swarmed with what were called "female missionary societies" by 1812, and by 1816 three Baptist wives, supported by these societies, were en route to Ceylon as missionaries. "If not deceived in our motives," one of them wrote, "we have been induced to leave our beloved friends and native shores to cross the tempestuous deep, from love to Christ and the souls which he died to purchase. And now we are ready, waiting with the humble hope of being employed, in his own time and way, in building up his kingdom."

I was surprised to learn that the Civil War strongly affected the progress of women in missions. It was an educative force in America, for through it women were driven to organize because of their pity for the fighting men and their patriotism. In the ten years following the war, scores of organizations, including many new missionary societies, were launched.

The nineteenth-century mind boggled at the thought of single women serving on a foreign field. A few widows were accepted, having supposedly profited by the guidance of husbands and therefore being more knowledgeable and dependable than single women could be expected to be. The first single woman on record who was sent to a foreign land was one Betsy Stockton and she was black.

Of Eleanor Macomber of Burma it was said, "No husband helped her decide the momentous question, and when she resolved, it was to go *alone*. With none to share her thousand cares and complexities, with no heart to keep time with the wild beatings of her own, she, a friendless woman, crossed the deep dark ocean, and on soil never trodden by the feet of Christian men, erected the banner of the Cross." This is typical of the sentimental view of missionaries which makes most of us cringe. This description was written by a man, but don't let his phrases "weak, defenseless woman" and "the wild beatings of her heart" blur the single fact of Eleanor Macomber's action. Don't stay home because you don't like the *image*. True faith is action. Faith cometh by hearing, and results in *doing*.

I could go on listing what women have done to prove that they have had an important role in world missions. There were Mary Slessor of Calabar, Lottie Moon of China, Amy

Carmichael of India, Rosalind Goforth of China, Malla Moe of Africa—of whom it was said that although she could not preach like Peter or pray like Paul, told thousands of the love of Jesus. And besides these names there have surely been tens of thousands of nameless nuns and other anonymous women who have done what God sent them to do—and they've done it without the tub-thumping of modern egalitarian movements. They had a place and they knew they had it because Scripture says they have.

You read in your Bible from Romans 12, "All members do not have the same function." There is nothing interchangeable about the sexes, and there is nothing interchangeable about Christians. God has given gifts that *differ*. They differ *according to the grace given to us*. You and I, whether we are men or women, have nothing to do with the choice of the gift. We have everything to do with the use of the gift.

There are diversities of operations, but the same Spirit. There are varieties of personalities, but all are made in the image of God. As a woman I find clear guidance in Scripture about my position in church and home. I find no exemption from the obligations of commitment and obedience. My obligations have certainly varied from time to time and from place to place. I started my missionary work as a single woman with three other single women. There was no church, there were no believers, and there were no male missionaries. Later I was a wife and had to rearrange certain priorities in accordance with what I understood to be my job, as a wife, as a co-worker with my husband in the field, and later as a mother.

When my husband was killed by Indians, I found myself in some indefinable positions. There wasn't one missionary man left in Ecuador at that time who spoke the jungle Quechua language. There was no one to teach the young Quechua Christians, no one to lead the church, no one but women to carry on where five missionary men had left off. The door to the Auca tribe had slammed shut for those men and was, to our astonishment, opened to two women. It didn't look to me like a woman's job but God's categories are not always ours. I had to shuffle my categories many times during my last eight years of missionary work. Since coming back to the States I've had a career of sorts, I've remarried and been widowed again.

But it is the same faithful Lord who calls me by name and never loses track of my goings and reminds us all in a still, small voice, "Ye are my witnesses that ye might know and believe me and understand that I am he." There's our primary responsibility; to *know him*. I can't be a witness unless I've seen something, unless I know what it is I am to testify to.

And it is the Lord of the universe who calls you—women and men—and offers you today a place in his program. Your education or lack of it, your tastes and prejudices and fears and ambitions, your age or sex or color or height or marital status or income bracket are all things which may be offered to God, after you've presented your bodies as a living sacrifice. And God knows exactly what to do with them. They're not obstacles if you hand them over. Be still and know that he is God. Sit in silence and wonder and expectancy, and never doubt that the Lord of your life has his own way of getting through to you to let you know the specifics of his will.

And if you know that you've seen something, you can add your voice to the host of witnesses like G. K. Chesterton who, in answer to the historical query of why Christianity was accepted, answers for millions of others: "Because it fits the lock; because it is like life. We are Christians not because we worship a key but because we have passed a door and felt the wind that is the trumpet of liberty blow over the land of the living."

Read on for an excerpt from Elisabeth Elliot's

These Strange Ashes

— 1 —

The Way In

It is unsettling to me now to know that people who are making a tour of South America can take a short, easy side trip and see the Colorados. They can go in a taxi from the city of Quito to Santo Domingo de los Colorados in a few hours and stay in a nice motel and have a look at a real Colorado Indian any day of the week. The Indians will even dance for you, I am told, or play their wonderful bamboo marimbas. This tells me that everything has changed. I expected things to change, but I did not expect them to change with such frightening speed. The Colorados did not want money twenty years ago. Not money or anything else back then would induce them to come out of hiding on a weekday into the white man's town to do what the white man wanted them to do. Some impression has been made on them, deeply and I am sure irreversibly, and they have been changed.

In the southwest part of North America you can see Indians doing things to amuse white people. There are still those who will "dress up" or dance or demonstrate pottery making or blanket weaving so the tourist will feel that he has been in "real

Indian country" and has seen the way Indians live. It has taken a hundred years to bring things to this state. In South America, things have moved much faster. White men, of course, have been there for hundreds of years but had not touched most of the jungle. Indigenous peoples kept on living as they had always lived right on up until the middle of the twentieth century. But then things happened in a moment, in the twinkling of an eye, and they have all been changed. What the tourist pays to see now—is it the Indian I saw?

Dorothy and I, both of us single, both Americans, both students of linguistics, she from Texas, I from New Jersey, rode to Santo Domingo on the tailgate of a pickup. It was no side trip on a vacation tour. Each of us had prayed for years for God's guidance to the place of His choice for our missionary work. We had lived together in a seventeen-dollar-a-month "walkup" in Brooklyn, New York, near a small church group of Puerto Ricans who offered us the free use of the apartment so that we could work with them and learn some Spanish. We were almost the only ones who spoke English in the neighborhood (Bushwick Avenue near what the conductor on the El called "Moitle Avenue"). There was heat in our apartment for a couple of hours a day, and we never knew which hours those would be. There was hot water usually between six and seven in the morning. The Rhinegold Brewery was right next door, and we smelled beer and listened to the noise of trucks all day and all night. There were rats—large black rats, big enough to dump over the garbage pail in the kitchen. It was probably good training for us, living there, and we learned a little Spanish, too. But it proved to be only a smattering, and when we got to Ecuador we spent another six months at it in the capital city of Quito, living in luxury in comparison with our Brooklyn situation, in the home of an educated white Ecuadorian couple who knew no English.

But at last it was time to turn from Spanish studies to the work at which we had been aiming for so long—work with an

Indian tribe whose language was yet unwritten. I hoped someday to reduce such a language to writing and translate the Bible. Two English women, untrained in linguistics, needed help in the Colorado tribe. They also badly needed someone to take charge of the school. Here was our chance.

We rode, as I said, on the tailgate of a pickup that belonged to a missionary whom everyone called ET who lived in Santo Domingo. He was a skinny, serious man in his thirties who seemed always to have time to spare, and, unlike most missionaries, never worried about money. He ran some sort of banana business along with his missionary work and spent a lot of time shuttling back and forth between the west jungle and the city. His wife Vera was, fortunately, an easygoing, good-humored woman who did more than her share of the missionary work and, I found out, sometimes went without eggs or some other minor luxury in order to pay off ET's business debts.

ET and Vera picked us up early one morning in September of 1952 for the day's journey down to Santo Domingo. We drove first around backstreets we didn't know existed, ET banging on wooden gates and high walls ("I've got to pick up a letter here"), buying truck parts in tiny alleyways ("I told a guy I'd get these for him"), chatting with slick, disreputable characters in dark banana storerooms. He had contacts. There was no doubt about that. "Señor Eduardo!" a woman called from an upstairs window, and came rushing down to the truck to hand him a packet. "For my sister, please, Señor Eduardo, this little favor!" We were supposed to "make the first chain." The road to Santo Domingo, ET had explained, was narrow and winding, and twice a day a chain was opened to allow traffic to pass through, going down to the jungle. There was a chain at the other end of the road that was closed to maintain one-way traffic. The "first chain" at our end was at nine o'clock in the morning, but we were still bumping around the cobblestones of Quito at eleven. ET had lived long enough in Ecuador to have learned (perhaps he always knew) how to shrug off the demands of time. Mañana was always good enough. The two o'clock chain would get us to Santo Domingo by midnight or a little before. We did not like any of this, but there was nothing we could do but sit on the tailgate (because the truck was fully loaded with assorted cargo) and go where we were taken.

Shortly after noon, ET finished his rounds. We began the long climb up out of the city, winding around the deep folds of the mountain called Pichincha, where Spanish conquistadores had fought the Incas, higher and higher until we saw the city lying spread out as in a vast bowl below us, velvet slopes on every side, snowcaps gleaming beyond. Quito had seemed to me, when I had first arrived there six months before, an exotic city where the race of time had been slowed nearly to a stop.

It was a Spanish colonial city founded in 1534 and retaining still a certain grace from the Old Word—whitewashed adobe houses lined narrow cobbled streets over which jutted carved balconies of lovely dark wood festooned with geraniums. There were delicate wrought iron gates with heavy handmade hinges and door knockers. The green squares and parks had fountains and statuary and some were bordered by graceful colonnades. In six months I had learned to love this city and thought of it as legendary, a city of the faraway and long ago, but as we looked back on it from the high mountain slopes on our way to the jungle, it seemed a last look at the twentieth century. Quito was civilization, and we were leaving it. I was leaving, too, a young man named Jim Elliot, who had studied Spanish with Dorothy and me. We had been acquainted in college, and in Quito he and his colleague, Pete, had lived across the street from Dorothy and me and had eaten two meals a day in the Arias house with us. Jim and I had walked in the pastures on the outskirts of town, had climbed Pichincha and seen the sun rise as the moon was setting over the city, had ridden the bus to the post office on many rainy afternoons, and had explored the byways of the old sections of town, practicing our Spanish on friendly shopkeepers and children. He was heading for the eastern jungle to work with the Quichua Indians, and I knew it would be a long time before I saw him or even heard from him, since we would be separated by the double cordillera of the Andes and communication was exceedingly slow.

The frontier lay before us. "Therefore have I set my face like a flint" were words from Isaiah that had held me steady when I first decided to go to Ecuador, and they held me steady this time as well. Obedience to God was the reason for this journey.

It was a good thing for me to remind myself of the reason because, on top of everything, it was really great fun. It was an adventure and held the thrill of adventure, and if I put my mind on the things set before rather than on the things that were behind, I had no sense whatever of gritting my teeth and doing a thing I disliked. It was the thing I was made for and I was full of gladness.

There were sheep in some of the velvet meadows, and cows, and an occasional horse with an Indian rider. Adobe farmhouses stood here and there in a sheltered hollow or on a hillside by a running brook, screened sometimes by a comb of eucalyptus trees that had been planted to break the tearing Andean winds. Each loop of the cobblestone road brought us higher up the shoulders of Pichincha, and gave us ever vaster views of endless plain and mountain that stretched away north, south, and east. Cayambe was the snowcap to the north, a rounded mass that dominated the famous Otavalo Valley where the Indians live who make wonderful copies of English and Scottish woolens. Antisana, a series of tremendous snowy humps, stood between us and the Amazon basin to the east. To the south towered the near-perfect cone of Cotopaxi, glistening white at the top, spreading out in broad, smooth, black slopes of volcanic ash.

In the village of San Juan, at an altitude of 11,000 feet, we waited for the chain to be opened. ET explained that the cars were counted at the far end, and the number was reported by radio to San Juan.

It was very cold. Heavy drizzle was falling, called the *páramo*, the name also given to the high-grass country where this drizzle is almost constant. Sharp wind was blowing and people from other waiting trucks were standing about, the men wearing wool ponchos pulled tightly about their necks and shoulders, the women covering their noses and mouths with heavy shawls. There was a little shack where we bought ears of hot steamed corn, fried potatoes, and hard-boiled eggs. The corn had huge, soft kernels and was sweet and delicious. We warmed our hands on it as we ate. There were Coca-Colas for sale, some blackened bananas, a mineral water call *Aqua Güitig*, and jars of biscuits and hard candy. A radio was turned to its loudest volume, giving forth the nasal, five-note songs of the Andean Indians, songs sung in Spanish but echoing the loneliness of the bleak mountain country, the lostness of a people stripped and despoiled.

Far down the valley on the western side of the mountains we could see the great cumbersome banana trucks laboring up the steep grade, disappearing into the folds of the ravine, winding into view again, up and up. The sound of the gears reached us faintly. At last they rumbled over the top, coasted down a slight grade into the village, and came to a halt at the chain. Papers were examined, the chain was opened, and they came through and stopped for their corn and eggs and drinks. We waited again. More trucks came. More waiting. The man at the chain decided—we supposed he had counted the reported number of trucks—that the moment had come to let us through. But it turned out that the man was not terribly particular in his count, for we had not gone far down the road when the truck in the front of our caravan came grill-to-grill with another truck on its way up.

"*Caramba*!" shouted the driver.

"*Caramba*!" shouted the other. "Don't you see that I'm on my way down?"

"Don't you see that I'm loaded?" And both drivers got out of their cabs, shouted, thrust clenched fists skyward, raved, and stamped. There were supposed to be unwritten rules of the road: the loaded truck had the right of way, or the truck going downhill had the right of way. If the truck going downhill met one that was loaded (which was certainly the most common kind of encounter), there was no one to arbitrate and long arguments became the rule. Everyone enjoyed these. They broke the monotony of the journey and gave everybody a chance to look over the crowd in the other vehicle. The drivers and "conductors," boys who usually rode on top of the load and were in charge of collecting fares and seeing to the baggage, loved the opportunity for oratory. Latin courtesies, subtleties, and passions were lavishly demonstrated, the passengers taking part as they felt inspired, and after a suitable interval a decision was reached. The orators leaped into the trucks, engines roared, and off they went again.

I had some idea of counting the horseshoe curves as we traveled. I could see eight or ten below us, but I soon realized the number was deceiving. The journey consisted of nothing but horseshoes, some of them cutting back into ravines much more deeply than appeared from above so that what looked like a single curve turned out to be three or four. The road was treacherous, without guardrails between us and the sheer chasms on one side. On the other side the mountain rose straight up, and at times we bumped across the remains of a landslide that had been mostly cleared from the road. Sometimes a waterfall sprayed our legs or even our heads as we sat on the bouncing tailgate. Once a banana truck coming behind us stopped just under a waterfall. The driver was absorbed in doing something, heedless of the furious shouts from the riders on top who were getting showered with ice water.

Most of the ravines had rivers in them, rushing, clear and joyful, from the heights and plummeting over the rock walls below. There were bridges in some places, but in others the river ran straight across the road and we drove through it. Dorothy and I, having no warning, of course got our feet wet.

The country was wilderness. We saw not more than twenty houses, even though we could see for miles and miles across canyons to the opposite slopes. It was as though we had been dropped into an uninhabited fold of the earth.

The flora changed as we traveled, from alpine meadows to jungle. The forest on the other side of the ravine we were skirting had a draped, stringy, humpy appearance because of the masses of vines and air plants that shrouded the trees. Here and there, there was the burst of a palm or a banana tree, but the general effect was weird and, to me, unearthly, being unlike anything in my own world. It was a journey into a strange dreamland—from the colorful city of Quito, where the gardens were bright with flowers and the white houses dazzled your eyes in the equatorial light, into this deep canyon of grotesqueries, wetness, and increasing gloom. Clouds swirled around us for a time, and then we found ourselves dropping below the clouds into a kind of misty twilight, finally into utter darkness as night fell and not a twinkle of light shone from any house or any star. A curtain had fallen. It was the end of one life. There was no sadness because of that ending, none at all that I remember now. There were both the hesitancy and the expectancy you feel when you have knocked on an unknown door. You do not know who will open it, or what you will see on the other side.

Late in the evening we found ourselves traveling at last over flat land. After all those miles of curves and steep inclines, it was as welcome as the sight of shore to a sailor. We passed through sugar cane and banana plantations. A wooden fence, a saddled and tethered horse, a tiny point of light, told us there must be houses nearby. Then we came to a few shops close by the road, with the din of radios and voices issuing from open doors. Life was being lived here, so far from civilization. People drank and sang in the shops, slept in the silent houses that we could not see behind the banana trees. Of the three foreigners who happened by on the road in the dark, one at least strained her eyes in imagination toward those unseen drinkers and singers and sleepers. "We've come. God has sent us, and we're here now. What will He do for us?"

— 2 —

A Missionary House

ET drove the pickup into the yard of his house. Dorothy and I got off the tailgate, rubbed our bruised derrières, and stumbled into the house, helping ET and Vera unload the stuff they had brought. There were wooden boxes nailed and bound with hemp, which Vera called "kerosene boxes," but not because they had kerosene in them now. There were sacks of staples such as flour, lentils, beans, and macaroni. There were enough machine parts to repair every gadget and tool and vehicle west of the Andes, which in fact ET probably intended to do. There were baskets of brightly enameled plates and cups, stainless steel spoons, aluminum kettles of graduated sizes, and there were steel drums of gasoline, sheets of corrugated roofing, and an old battered suitcase. The house was totally dark, but Vera lit two small kerosene lamps—*lamparillas* they are called—and as my eyes became adjusted to the dim light I saw that the house that they called home was a hovel. The missionaries I had known in Quito lived in pleasant, comfortable adobe houses with whitewashed walls and polished wood or tile floors. They had furniture, rugs, and pictures. I expected jungle missionaries to live differently, but not this differently. A grass hut, natural and harmonious and fitting in these surroundings, would not have shocked me. But here was squalor. The house was a sketchy wooden structure, unpainted, and so far as I could tell in the dim light, black. There seemed to be four rooms, each opening into the next, with no hallways or center. Vera told Dorothy and me which was ours, pointed out laughingly that there was no door on it or on any of the other rooms, only curtains for privacy. "Don't mind us, we're just Grand Central Station here!" she said, and for a second I wished I could catch the next train. We found our way to bed.

The next day we had a better look around. The house was indeed black—unpainted wood that had blackened with the dampness and mildew. There were four children who appeared to belong to ET and Vera, though no introductions were made and the children did not seem to speak much English. One or two other people who apparently lived in the house spoke no English. Where they all slept remained a mystery—we had one of the bedrooms, there was a sort of kitchen-living room, and we assumed the other two curtains hid bedrooms. The house was furnished with the barest essentials of tables and chairs or benches of shoddy construction, and Vera cooked on a *fogón*, a sort of sandbox on legs with a fire built on it. Smoke filled the house.

I wanted to get out of this place. The depression it brought me made me feel guilty, for I thought at the time that the ugliness and squalor and lack of privacy were sacrifices appropriate for a servant of the Lord. If I did not like the atmosphere it must mean that I was not yet prepared to lay down my life as I had promised.

The children depressed me. They ought to have spoken to a guest in English, but they spoke hardly at all and always in Spanish. They looked peaked and grubby, they wore no shoes, and their clothes hung on their thin little frames in a most pathetic way. Urchins they were, like their only friends, the town urchins. "Identification" was the idea, I told myself, and it seemed a good principle, but when I saw this demonstration of it in practice something seemed awry.

The yard around the house was practically bald of grass—there were a few tufts in the fence corners, but the rest was slick, hard-packed mud covered with a greenish, scabby crust. There was an outhouse used by the family, a crazy, tall shack emitting a most lethal effluvium, but a steady parade of townspeople were making use of an empty lot next door as a bathroom. They were not seeking privacy, that was obvious, but only space, and judging by the caution with which they stepped, there was little enough of that remaining.

I persuaded Dorothy to go out for a walk. Vera was busy in the kitchen and said she did not need our help. Visitors were coming and going, some of them helping Vera, some of them talking, asking for things, bringing things, the children were in and out, ET was hammering on something. I wanted only to get out of all this for a little while.

We wandered through Santo Domingo de los Colorados. The place looked like a set for a Hollywood western. There was a big, empty square, or *plaza*, mostly of mud, in the center of town, which had a few feeble cannas, a banana tree with shredded leaves, and a scraggly palm trying its best to grow. Wooden buildings faced the square, thatched or roofed with rusted, corrugated iron, the roofs extended to form a covered walkway. The shop doors were wide open, the wares stacked and festooned in the doorways in a jumble of color and tawdriness. The streets were sloughs of deeply rutted mud with standing pools of water. On one side of the *plaza* a row of banana trucks was parked. Men were loading bananas into them from the backs of mules and donkeys and from wooden carts. They were American trucks, I could see from the make of the hoods, but ungainly wooden bodies had been built onto the chassis, and painted bright blue, bright red, pink, yellow, and green, and decorated with pictures, curlicues, mottoes, and names such as "Hitler," "Mother of God," "Little Angel," "The Bull," or "Sacred Heart of Jesus." I came to realize later the huge importance of these trucks. They were the very heart and life of the western jungle. A man might go into terrible debt for many years in order to buy one, and when he had it, he gave himself to it with utter slavish devotion. He named it, first of all, giving it a name of power and protection. This "bull" or "mother of God" would call forth all of his courage and strength and love and would in turn transport and support him, enable and ennoble him, and make him powerful and influential and capable of moving people, of lifting up one and putting down another. There would be no town of Santo Domingo de los Colorados if there were no trucks, and the mayor himself was, like everybody, at the mercy of the truck drivers.

In addition to the pickup we had come down in, ET had a banana truck. It was a big one, painted and named, although I have forgotten what name he gave it—perhaps "The Evangelist." As time went on, it appeared that ET had a great many things going besides his missionary work. In fact, there seemed to be less of the missionary business than met the eye. He had a way of picking up odd jobs here and there, dubious as profit-making pursuits but very profitable, he claimed, as "contacts." A missionary is supposed to make contacts, to get acquainted with people in order to give them his message, and there are many byways. As to the question of legal permission to conduct business on a missionary's visa, ET was not at all bothered. The Lord took care of the details.

Dorothy and I did the whole town in an hour. It was not much of a place. It had little of interest and nothing whatever of beauty. I could not help admitting to myself that I was deeply thankful that God had not appointed me to work here. ET and Vera, apparently, were the appointees, and I was glad of that.

Elisabeth Elliot (1926–2015) was one of the most perceptive and popular Christian writers of the last century. The author of more than twenty books, including *Passion and Purity*, *The Journals of Jim Elliot*, and *These Strange Ashes*, Elliot offered guidance and encouragement to millions of readers worldwide. For more information about Elisabeth's books, visit ElisabethElliot.org.